Just Leave God Out of It

Just Leave God Out of It

Cultural Compromises We Make

TIM RITER
AND
DAVID TIMMS

Building the New Generation of Believers

An Imprint of Cook Communications Ministries
COLORADO SPRINGS, COLORADO • PARIS, ONTARIO
KINGSWAY COMMUNICATIONS, LTD., EASTBOURNE, ENGLAND

NexGen® is an imprint of
Cook Communications Ministries, Colorado Springs, CO 80918
Cook Communications, Paris, Ontario
Kingsway Communications, Eastbourne, England

JUST LEAVE GOD OUT OF IT
© 2004 by Tim Riter and David Timms

First Printing, 2004
Printed in the United States of America
1 2 3 4 5 6 7 8 9 10 Printing/Year 08 07 06 05 04

ISBN: 0781440564

To the emerging generations, including my own three sons (Matthew, Caleb, and Joel), who will find these values of the kingdom both immensely countercultural and immensely freeing, if embraced. To Tim (my cowriter) for pushing me forward when I was a slow starter. Lastly, to Kim, who does more to hold these kingdom values before me than anyone else I know.

D. T.

To Fritz Moga and Travis Twyman, part of the group that birthed this idea. Thanks for your love of God, your understanding of his Word, and for being fellow followers of Jesus. And to David, I literally couldn't have done this without you, my friend!

T. R.

CONTENTS

Introduction
    God's Values Confront the Twenty-First Century. 9

Part 1 Attitudes Toward God

Chapter 1 **Just Leave God Out of It**
    Secularism Clashes with Supernaturalism 17

Chapter 2 **Who Are You to Tell Me What to Do?**
    Relativism Clashes with Absolute Truth 29

Chapter 3 **Pick a Path, Any Path, to God**
    Pluralism Clashes with Jesus. 39

Part 2 Attitudes Toward Others

Chapter 4 **It's All About Me!**
    Self-Centeredness Clashes with Service. 51

Chapter 5 **I Don't Need Your Help**
    Independence Clashes with Interdependence 61

Chapter 6 **Winning Isn't Everything; It's the Only Thing**
    Competition Clashes with Cooperation. 73

Chapter 7 **Just Do It!**
    Sexual Freedom Clashes with Purity 83

Chapter 8 **Whatever Makes You Happy**
    Tolerance Clashes with Tough Love 93

Part 3 Attitudes Toward Self

Chapter 9 **I Want It and I Want It Now**
    Instant Satisfaction Clashes
    with Delayed Gratification 105

Chapter 10 **But It Feels So Good**
   Pleasing Self (Hedonism) Clashes with Sacrifice..... 115

Chapter 11 **You *Will* Do What I Say**
   Power Clashes with Submission................. 125

Chapter 12 **Whatever Works**
   Pragmatism Clashes with Obedience.............. 133

Chapter 13 **The Sky Is My Limit**
   Ambition Clashes with Honoring God 143

Part 4   Attitudes Toward Life

Chapter 14 **What's the Score?**
   Success Clashes with Faithfulness 153

Chapter 15 **Show Me the Money!**
   Accumulation Clashes with Giving 161

Chapter 16 **One for the Road**
   Consumerism Clashes with Simplicity............. 171

Chapter 17 **I'll Get to It When I Get to It**
   Laziness Clashes with Diligence.................. 183

Chapter 18 **Life Sucks**
   Pessimism Clashes with Optimism................ 193

Chapter 19 **What Will Be Will Be**
   Determinism Clashes with Our Choice............ 203

NexStep.. 217

Introduction

God's Values Confront the Twenty-First Century

In 1999, David attended a men's retreat at a bush camp outside Sydney, Australia. Saturday morning had been devoted to studies about prayer, so lunchtime called for a change of pace. Soon a large group was playing touch rugby (football to those from the States). Without warning, a fifty-year-old dentist fell to the ground, holding his ankle and gasping in pain. His foot dangled, and it wasn't long before we realized he'd seriously damaged his Achilles tendon.

The caring group of men rushed to his aid, ran for ice, and began to determine the quickest way to transport him to the hospital. A camp worker, attracted by the commotion, saw the crowd and hurried over. When he saw the problem, his simple question convicted them all: "Has anyone prayed for him yet?"

Ouch! Great and intense teachings that morning on prayer, ignored. So they prayed ... and then rushed him to the hospital.

This incident highlights what we call "cultural creep." Much like the cholesterol that slowly clogs our arteries until the fatal heart attack strikes, so we remain oblivious to the secular values that stealthily take hold of us. And without realizing it, we absorb those values. This compromises, confuses, and frustrates us as we try to live out our faith.

Think with us about conflicting values. Values of the culture tell us to get medical attention—quickly. Scriptural values tell us to pray about everything. No problem. Unless we ignore one. The prime one. The need to pray. Please don't think we advocate praying only and avoiding medical care. Not at all. But neither should we neglect prayer and just get medical care.

This challenge is serious. The values of our culture subtly squeeze us into their mold, at the expense of biblical values. David's experience at the bush camp highlights how easily that can happen to us. George Barna reports that 75 percent of all American evangelical Christians reject absolute truth. How can we believe in God and at the same time dismiss the concept of absolute truth? The confusion and potential compromise is obvious.

What happens when secular and godly values clash? When the values of the kingdom of God contradict the values of the world, which do we follow? How do we discern the differences? This book addresses those issues and helps followers of Jesus identify the differences, live in accord with God's values, and become gracious and effective agents of change.

Make no mistake: we must wrestle daily with incompatible value systems. Tim remembers a nationally known speaker who suggested that when we face a life decision, we decide what we'd normally do, then do the opposite! Why? God says, "My thoughts are not your thoughts, neither are your ways my ways" (Isa. 55:8). It may not be a good policy on every occasion, but it certainly highlights the struggle we face.

Jesus made it clear that we must simultaneously engage the world yet remain different from it. He said to his Father, "My prayer is not that you take them out of the world but that you protect them from the evil one. They are not of the world, even as I am not of it" (John 17:15–16). Later, Peter exhorted us to live as aliens in the world (see 1 Peter 2:11) because we cannot share its values.

Jesus wants us in the world as effective and gracious change agents. But too often, we're *changed* agents—changed by our contact with the world. We're more influenced than influencing. J. B. Phillips translated Romans 12:2 this way: "Don't let the world around you squeeze you into its own mould, but let God re-make you so that your whole attitude of mind is changed."

How do we resist the constant pressure to buy into the world's values? How do we identify subtle and destructive values? What is the biblical countervalue? How do we let God change our thoughts, values, and behaviors?

Life-giving values start with a love for God. When asked about the greatest commandment, Jesus replied, "'Love the Lord your God with all your heart and with all your soul and with all your mind.' This is the first and greatest commandment. And the second is like it: 'Love your neighbor as yourself'" (Matt. 22:37–39).

Jesus' greatest commandment provides the structure for this book. First, we'll look at the cultural values that threaten our relationship with God. Second, we'll explore the cultural values that undermine our relationship and attitudes toward others. Third, we'll examine the cultural values that diminish our attitudes toward self. Finally, as we tie it all together, we'll contemplate the cultural values that diminish life itself.

Why are God's values so important? Several decades ago, Tim traveled with a group on a mission project to a small village outside Taos, New Mexico. He and a friend, Chris, rode motorcycles. Tim's was a stock 750 Honda. He rode it to Taos, then to visit family in Nashville, Tennessee, and back home to California. On a trip of over 5,000 miles, the only problem with the bike was a piece of grit that clogged the carburetor jet; half an hour of work fixed it.

Chris's bike was a beautiful custom chopper that won first place in the Winternational motorcycle show that year. But fifty miles outside Flagstaff, Arizona, the rear tire blew. The tightly molded rear fender slightly scraped the tire, and Chris discovered that what looked so good in the showroom didn't work so well on the highway. Later, the battery became so overheated that Chris couldn't sit on the seat. He made it to Taos, but halfway home, the bike was so problem-ridden he had to have it hauled the rest of the way in a pickup truck.

Think about the implications. Honda hires expert engineers to design a bike, and they do it well. But some guy wants to customize it, so he extends the forks with a springer suspension. Then he adds a peanut gas tank with concealed wiring and a molded rear fender. It looks good, but it doesn't perform on the road. Why? It moved beyond the expert's original design.

God created us. He knows how we function best and what values lead to the most satisfying life. Then we tweak things just a little. "Yeah, I know God said ... but ..." Our reasoning makes sense to us, and it works. For a while. But when we change the values that God designed for optimum life, when we deviate from the expert's original design, sooner or later, as our values break down, so do our lives.

Just Leave God Out of It will help you understand the difference between the values of the Master Designer and those of the master imposter. You'll see how God has designed our lives to work and to work well. Grapple with these issues. Work through them. Don't blindly accept what the culture says is best. Be discerning. Seek God's best. And join us in being gracious change agents, effective in telling people about the values that lead to life.

Part One

Attitudes Toward God

Chapter One

Just Leave God Out of It

Secularism Clashes with
Supernaturalism

David has three young boys. Joel, the youngest at just three years old, likes to play hide-and-seek. If he hasn't had time to hide well, however, he simply covers his eyes, presuming he becomes instantly invisible. (All three-year-olds do this.) He assumes that if he can't see his dad, then his dad can't see him. It is childish—and it is foolish—and we do it all the time with God.

Ravi Zacharias, in his provocative book *Deliver Us from Evil*, wrote, "Simply stated, secularism asserts that public life is to be conducted without reference to religion or to any notion of transcendence." In essence, our culture, which is based on secularism, urges us to live our public lives as though God does not exist.

The separation of God from our culture is so complete that we now describe America as a post-Christian culture—joining the rest of the western world. Although some polls indicate that 40 percent of adult Americans attend church during a typical week, look at the evidence for secularism.

Las Vegas is currently the fastest-growing city in the United States. Over the past ten years, nearly 200 new people per day have moved to greater Las Vegas. Kevin Odor, senior pastor of the 3500-member Canyon Ridge Christian Church in northwest Vegas, said to David, "Every week thousands of people seeking God fill the churches in Las Vegas. They come to the city seeking tax shelters, good luck, quick money, or business opportunities. And many of these people now realize they need to seek God. But a large number of them have never heard the name of Jesus Christ in any form but profanity, have never opened a Bible or heard a Bible story, and have no idea of the Judeo-Christian heritage of our western culture."

We see this outside of Las Vegas as well.

When George W. Bush gave his inaugural address in January 2001, Dick Meyer of *CBS News* confessed, "There were a few phrases in the speech I just didn't get. One was, 'When we see that wounded traveler on the road to Jericho, we will not pass to the other side.'" Meyer concluded, "I hope there's not a quiz." He did not recognize the allusion to Jesus' story about the Good Samaritan (see Luke 10).

This cultural separation runs much deeper than banning prayer from schools or removing "under God" from the Pledge of Allegiance. Ignorance of Christian values and the Bible abounds, and the wedge between God and culture results from secularism driving western culture.

CULTURE'S VALUE

What It Is

Secularism tends to operate at two levels. The first level flatly denies that God exists. The atheist rejects any notion of God and asserts that what we see is all there is. The more subtle second level acknowledges that God or a Supreme Being exists, but it denies his involvement in the world. In the past, we called this deism. In practical terms, however, atheism and deism possess few differences. They both agree that this material world is all we have.

The moment we admit to a transcendent Being, however, and, more importantly, acknowledge God's presence and participation in our world, we have to make a choice: we either yield to him or we rebel against him. If we agree that God is active among us, we can reasonably assume that we should live in a way pleasing to him, given our lesser status.

It's for Real

Katie told her girlfriends, all college students, about a recent encounter. Her boyfriend had spent the night in her room at her parents' house, and the next morning they confronted her about it. "Katie, we don't want you sleeping with your boyfriend, especially in our house. It offends God." Her response? "Gosh, Mom and Dad! This is the twenty-first century. Just leave God out of it."

Charles Colson suggested that the collapse of the U.S. energy giant Enron was an inevitable result of modern secularism. When business executives dismiss the values of the kingdom of God and adopt secular values, chaos and collapse follow. The unraveling of corporate America—Enron, WorldCom, MCI, Tyco, and Adelphia—testifies to the pervasive influence of secularism, the systematic denial of a Higher One to whom we are accountable.

Caught in this ethical vacuum, Harvard Business School stopped teaching ethics and returned a $20 million endowment to the benefactor because secularism, which has determined their curriculum in recent times, provides no acceptable basis for ethics. Even the "No Child Left Behind" Act passed by the U.S. government underscores a foundationless cultural value system when it instructs all school curriculum to be "secular, neutral, and nonideological." We cannot doubt that secularism has permeated our culture.

The Payoffs

The benefits of excluding God and embracing secularism are obvious. We become completely free agents, able to do what we like. If we dismiss God, we believe we are not subject to his authority or his judgment. Put simply, no higher authority, no higher responsibility, and no higher obligation exceeds ourselves. We decide the rules by which we will live. We set our own code of ethics.

Secularists usually warm to rationalism and science. They comfortably explain life in terms of physics, chemistry, or psychology. No loose ends. Nothing exceeds the human capacity to understand. Then, with knowledge comes inflated feelings of power and superiority.

Secularists also put on a pedestal human emotions and

personal preferences. If God has lesser authority, we can do what pleases us. Individual feelings and desires become our primary guide.

In a clever smoke-and-mirrors act, secularism elevates human beings to the highest place in the universe. The denial of the supernatural makes the natural realm the highest one. And since we reside at the top of the natural realm, we rule the universe. It feels good, even if the foundation is wobbly.

The Costs

Secularism comes at a profound personal cost. Ironically, while secularism elevates humanity, it undermines personal fulfillment.

Blaise Pascal, a seventeenth-century mathematician and theologian, wrote that a "God-shaped void" exists within every human being. Today, we seek to fill that vacuum with various material and emotional alternatives. But only God can satisfy that longing, and personal emptiness inevitably results from embracing the non-God worldview of our day.

In the blockbuster movie *Signs*, a pastor loses his wife in a tragic accident and abandons his belief in God. He tells his brother, "We're all alone here. No one to help us out." He concludes that good outcomes are just coincidences, not signs of God's involvement in the world. Yet it's not long before the pastor finds himself unable to live with the practice of secularism because it gives rise to feelings of profound aloneness. The human heart yearns to be known and to be loved.

That's really no surprise, because God created us for fellowship and love. Ultimately, then, the richest and most unconditional love we can experience comes from our heavenly Father. Secularism—living without reference to God—deprives us of that relational experience for which he created us. It exacerbates feelings of emptiness and produces disconnectedness and isolation.

Tragically, the rise of secularism coincides with the demise of values and culture. The judicial system and police force seek to enforce "community standards" among us, but who determines those standards? The courts now say that they are shaped by what the culture accepts. They don't impose the standards of the minority but reflect the views of the majority. And utter chaos emerges.

In 2001, Rene Rivkin, a flamboyant Sydney financier, sued the *Sydney Morning Herald* for defamation. The *Herald's* lawyer argued that even if the news article in question did imply that Rivkin, a married man with five children, had sex with his male chauffeur, there would be "no defamatory consequences as far as the plaintiff's reputation is concerned. Our community nowadays and for some time does not regard it as wrong … in the sense as worthy of condemnation … [and it is] now conduct widely accepted in the community." The lawsuit was dismissed.

At about the same time, the courts in a similar manner almost dismissed the case of a woman who had been raped. Their reasoning? "She's just a prostitute." When there is no authority higher than self, the loudest and most persistent voices within society determine its values. What a slippery slope! Monica Lewinsky's fellation of a president did not turn her into a social outcast; rather, she became the most sought-after, A-list party guest on the planet. In March 2001, *New York* magazine ran the cover headline "Monica Takes Manhattan." As one columnist noted: "The only lasting consequence of Zippergate was that graphic sexual details became commonplace in previously polite newspapers."

GOD'S VALUE

What It Is

The Bible opens with these strategic words: "In the beginning God...." At the beginning of any discussion of values or ethics, we have to decide about God. Many worldviews, including secularism, begin with humanity or culture or tradition or philosophy. But the Bible makes it clear that the starting point must be God himself.

The word *supernatural* may confuse us because we tend to hear it as *extraordinary, fanciful, invisible,* or *unreal.* God teaches the exact opposite. In speaking about the end of this "natural" world, Paul promised, "Now we see things imperfectly as in a poor mirror, but then we will see everything with perfect clarity. All that I know now is partial and incomplete, but then I will know everything completely, just as God knows me now" (1 Cor. 13:12 NLT).

Doesn't that suggest that this material world in which we live is a pale reflection of the perfect world God intended? The spiritual realm provides the greater reality. As the apostle Paul reminded his Athenian audience, "In him we live and move and have our being" (Acts 17:28). The reality of God directs all we do.

Dallas Willard writes,

> God did not start to bring his kingdom into existence through Jesus' presence on earth. The gospel concerned only the new accessibility of the kingdom to humanity through Jesus. So, when Jesus directs us to pray, "Thy kingdom come," he does not mean we should pray for it to come into existence. Rather, we pray for it to take over at all points in the personal, social, and political order where it is now excluded.... You cannot call upon Jesus Christ or upon God and *not* be heard. You live in their house, their *ecos* (Heb. 3:4). We usually call it simply "the universe." But they fully occupy it. It is their place, their "kingdom," where through their kindness and sacrificial love we can make our present life an eternal life.

The choice to live as kingdom-people starts with a choice for God and his kingdom. That decision will change our lives.

It's for Real

We base this book on the conviction that secularism is both misguided and destructive. We live in a supernatural context, whether or not we acknowledge it. God *does* love us, and he prescribes the way to abundant life. The kingdom of God is not an association we join, but a new worldview where we are aware of the presence of God, empowered by the Spirit of God, and seek the will of God. This, by the way, is not your fundamentally secular Sunday religion, which fails to include God in the day-to-day, hour-by-hour living. Kingdom living is altogether different.

We have to make a choice, right here and now. Do we embrace the secular stance of our day, excluding God from the marketplace, the school, and the workplace? Or do we choose the kingdom of God? We cannot have it both ways. And no workable alternatives exist.

The Payoffs

Living God's way in God's "house," as Willard puts it, ultimately produces liberation and exhilaration in all of life. God created us as body, soul, and spirit, according to 1 Thessalonians 5:23: "May God himself, the God of peace, sanctify you through and through. May your whole *spirit, soul and body* be kept blameless at the coming of our Lord Jesus Christ" (emphasis added). Did you notice all three parts? These biblical words describe our basic makeup.

If we deny our "spirituality," as secularists do, we deny something fundamental to our existence. As we open our lives to the reality of the supernatural realm, however, we discover life at a higher plane. The pursuit of God leads us to fulfillment. Additionally, we not only discover new power for living, but a whole new way of seeing the world.

A wonderful freedom comes when we see the world in its reality. No longer do we see a plain two-dimensional photograph but an enthralling three-dimensional landscape. Once we notice the 3-D picture, its depth and richness make everything else look flat. In short, our pursuit of God opens us to the fullness of ourselves and the fullness of reality.

The Costs

This countercultural pathway is not easy. Jesus told his disciples that the way is broad that leads to destruction and the way is narrow that leads to life (see Matt. 7:13–14). So, choosing God's way makes us swim against the tide. It contradicts everything that comes to us naturally, as well as the basic ethos of Western culture today. Jesus declared, however, "Blessed are those who have been persecuted for the sake of righteousness, for theirs is the kingdom of heaven" (Matt. 5:10 NASB). The blessing exceeds the high cost.

But when we choose to pursue rather than to deny God, richness touches the everyday fabric of our lives. Living life fully aware of and responsive to the supernatural realm is radical and powerful. Maybe we are no longer captains of our own fate, but we discover that the real Captain makes our future secure.

LIVING IT OUT

Nearly 350 years ago, a man known as Brother Lawrence entered a French monastery. He resolved that he would seek God in the ordinary, everyday demands of the monastery. So he volunteered to wash pots and pans—a menial activity. In the midst of the grease and grime, however, he learned to worship the "Lord of all pots and pans and things." Even washing dishes was not separate from the supernatural.

If we live fully aware of the supernatural realm, we will

discover God in the everyday. The secularist says that God is not involved in day-to-day affairs. Perhaps God shows up on Sundays, at weddings, maybe at funerals—or even in a crisis. The supernaturalist says we can never get away from God. He always goes before us. He always watches over us and participates in life with us.

Even doing laundry can, therefore, be a spiritual experience, as can mowing the grass. It all depends on our perspective. Laundry may help us picture God's cleansing grace—so we give thanks for his grace and forgiveness as we wash. Cutting grass may remind us of how God shapes our lives to produce beauty and order out of chaos. Change the perspective and you change the motivation. It ultimately changes the entire experience.

The film *Chariots of Fire* tells the story of two gifted runners in the 1924 Olympics in France. Harold Abrahams, the secularist, ran for personal glory. Eric Liddell, the Christian Scotsman, viewed his running in spiritual terms. Moments before Abrahams races in the 100-meter event, he says to a friend, "I have ten seconds in which to prove the reason for my existence, and even then, I am not sure I will." For him, running had no connection to God, and even winning would leave him empty.

Liddell, on the other hand, shared a different perspective with his sister prior to the 400-meter race. "Jenny, God has made me for a purpose—for China. But he has also made me fast. And when I run, I feel his pleasure." For Liddell, running connected him to God. The gold medal was incidental.

If we agree that God is active in our world, then we oblige

ourselves to accept his values as authoritative. When we embrace God and follow Christ it adds meaning and enrichment to every activity and relationship of life. But this choice (which you need to resolve before going any further in this book) is a countercultural, life-changing, watershed moment. The implications and consequences of your decision will provide the foundation for the rest of this book—and the rest of your life.

Chapter Two

Who Are You to Tell Me What to Do?

Relativism Clashes with Absolute Truth

The movie *All the Pretty Horses* opens with two young Texas cowboys watching the evening stars and grappling with truth. Lacy Rawlins asks, "You ever think about dying?"

Matt Damon's character, John Grady, replies, "Yeah, you?"

"Yeah, some."

"You think there's a heaven?"

"Yeah. Don't you?"

"I don't know. Yeah, maybe."

"Can you believe there's a heaven if you don't believe in hell?"

Then, setting up the theme of the movie, Grady replies, "I guess you can believe what you want to."

Grady expresses the relativism of our day. Each individual can determine such consequential truths as eternal life, heaven, and hell. But that concept comes back to haunt Grady and Rawlins. They head for Mexico to become working cowboys on a large ranch but first ride with a young kid who loses his horse in a thunderstorm, then steals it back.

They go their own way, but the police arrest the young cowboy and our two heroes join him in jail. A Mexican police captain asserts the kid never owned the horse, and Grady replies, "You have it your own ignorant way. As far as I know, that horse is his."

The policeman replies, "That is not the facts. We can make the truth here or we can lose it here. In three days, you will be in the hands of other people. Who's to say what the truth will be then?"

The captain did nothing but express Grady's original belief: truth is what you want to believe. Grady now disagrees: "There ain't but one truth. Truth is what happened, not what comes out of somebody's mouth."

Grady learned that truth doesn't always depend on our choices. Our desires don't determine truth. At this point we encounter one of the chief struggles our culture has with Christianity: the belief that some things are always true, regardless of our acceptance.

We believe that only through Jesus can we gain forgiveness, a relationship with the Father, and entry to heaven. And what do we hear from our culture? "Who are you to tell me what to believe? I'm a decent person. If God exists, he won't keep me out of heaven."

More than disagreeing with heaven's entrance requirements,

we clash over truth. Are some things always true? Or may we always believe what we want?

CULTURE'S VALUE

Merriam-Webster's Collegiate Dictionary (tenth edition) defines relativism as "a view that ethical truths depend on the individuals and groups holding them." Each individual or group establishes moral standards that become true and binding for them, even if not for anyone else.

We often hear in our culture, "You need to do what's true for you" or "Be true to yourself" or "Whatever you think." This view that individuals establish truth permeates our culture. That is relativism.

It's for Real

For twenty years, radio talk show host Dennis Prager asked high school seniors whom they'd save if both their dog and a stranger were drowning. Consistently, one-third voted for the dog, one-third for the stranger, and one-third couldn't answer.

When Prager asked the students who voted to save the person, "Were the students who voted to save the dog wrong?" the typical response was, "Listen, I personally feel that I should save the person, but they feel they should save their dog." No one *ever* said the decision to save the dog and not the person was wrong.

Relativism also permeates the church. In 1994, Josh McDowell surveyed 3,800 teens—80 percent attended evangelical churches; 86 percent said they'd committed their lives to Christ. Over 3,200 of the teens said right and wrong are subjective (relative), while nearly half said, "Everything in life is negotiable." These teenagers, many of whom are now parents, believe that each individual has the right personally to decide right from wrong, as long as it doesn't hurt anyone else. Consequently, lying is okay if it hurts no one *or* if it helps someone. Stealing is fine if the victim is either a corporation or government, but not an individual. Adultery is okay as long as both parties are stuck in bad marriages.

A recent George Barna survey indicated that only 28 percent of Americans strongly believe in absolute truth. The same survey revealed that only 23 percent of evangelicals expressed strong belief in absolute truth. Relativism thrives even more in the church than in our culture.

The Payoffs

Relativism offers enticing benefits and advantages.

First, it *respects individuality.* No one gets pushed into a box. We can express our uniqueness as persons. One size doesn't fit all. We are free to be ourselves, to determine our own drumbeat. Nobody tells us what to do.

Second, relativism *encourages personal preferences.* Many decisions in life have no absolutely right answer. What is the best flavor of ice cream? Which presidential candidate will make the best president? Is green a better color than blue? Relativism seems like a natural extension of such everyday choices, even when those decisions spill over to ethical issues. We appreciate the luxury of personal preferences so much that we demand the same on moral issues.

Third, relativism *rejects legalism.* This appeals to a culture that has grown suspicious and rebellious against established institutions, even Christian ones. Christians have a reputation as judgmental and legalistic, often over fairly minor issues. Relativism allows us to dismiss such people without needing to justify ourselves. We simply reject their views because we choose to. End of discussion.

The Costs

Relativism, however, has become an expensive luxury. When any society abandons a common set of values, *cultural disintegration* quickly follows. Despite the scorn often heaped on the "Ozzie and Harriet" decade of the 1950s, our culture had a common set of values that held us together. We've lost that bond, and we now struggle for a source of common identity. Relativism muddies personal values and contributes to cultural disintegration.

Brian and Jasmine, a young couple that Tim married, moved to a new community and got deeply involved in a local church. At the time, the couple didn't realize that the church took a lax view of the homosexual lifestyle. When Brian and Jasmine learned of it and talked to the pastor, he freely admitted that committed lesbian couples had full access to all leadership roles in the church. That prompted a struggle for this young couple. Were they out of touch, or was the pastor? Brian, who came from the Roman Catholic Church, yearned to go back to his roots, saying, "At least there you have one person who tells you what's right and wrong!" Institutional relativism confused the values of the individuals exposed to it.

Last, the logical extension of relativism is *anarchy*. When each individual establishes ethical values, only the strong survive. Relativism ultimately relies on the goodwill of each person to make ethical choices that don't harm others. And "right" becomes whatever we can get away with. The nation of Israel experienced this kind of anarchy. The last verse of Judges tells us, "In those days Israel had no king; everyone did as he saw fit" (21:25). The outcomes for the nation were chaos and division.

We must recognize the implications of relativism for our marriages and families, too. Disintegration, confusion, chaos, and division are guaranteed wherever relativism reigns.

GOD'S VALUE

What It Is

The concept of absolute truth permeates the Bible. We find, not suggestions, but commands. God views certain attitudes and acts as inherently wrong. We see God's foundational assumption that some things are always true.

God's truth offers security. It is forever reliable. Remember Grady's final comment? "There ain't but one truth. Truth is what happened, not what comes out of somebody's mouth."

Truth flows from God. He doesn't change the rules on us. We know what he values. Let's examine how absolute truth is imbedded in scripture.

It's for Real

God created reality. He, therefore, stands as the source of absolute truth. Not long ago Tim created a small wood project, but he didn't quite like how it turned out and trashed it. Why could he do that? Because he created it. We all recognize Genesis 1:1: "In the beginning God created the heavens and the earth."

Relativism flows from the premise that our minds are limited in what they *can* and *do* know, so we dare not pronounce an absolute. However, neither God's mind nor his knowledge are limited, so relativism doesn't apply to God. He can legitimately express absolute principles and rules to govern the reality he created.

Nevertheless, we retain the privilege of choice. We can reject God's absolutes, and we can still express preferences and opinions. In the area of moral or ethical truth, however, God has provided the non-negotiable blueprint for success. And that blueprint involves absolute moral principles. We jokingly say God gave the Ten Commandments, not the Ten Suggestions. Why? We recognize the authority behind them; they're not relative. To accept or reject them leads to serious consequences.

Jesus expected obedience to his commands. He said, "If you love me, you will obey what I command" (John 14:15). He did not invite discussion or debate. No negotiation. We can't modify his absolute commands.

What, then, are those absolutes? Perhaps we should begin with the creation accounts of Genesis 1–3. We find there God's original plan. We discover, for example, that human life is sacred because God made us in his image (see Gen. 1:27). Marriage is sacred because God ordained it (see Gen. 2:23–24). God created one woman for the man, not a harem. So, faithfulness to one person becomes a moral virtue. Since the center of the story deals with the broken relationship between humanity and God, the first moral requirement for life is to restore that relationship. If we're out of step with God, we'll be out of moral step in other areas, too.

We can draw many more absolutes from the creation narratives. This brief study shows that moral absolutes exist and come from God as the Creator of life.

The Payoffs

Our acceptance of God's absolutes produces *clear core values and direction*. We know what's right and wrong. We have clear boundaries. We may not always follow them perfectly, but we know them!

When we adhere to God's absolutes by adhering first to God himself, we discover the richness and fullness of life he intended. After all, as the designer, he knows what it takes.

Not only do we experience personal enrichment as we embrace God's way, but his blueprint provides the *foundation for unity and harmony between us*. It reestablishes our true identity as children of God and provides values that produce a common, consistent, and dependable foundation. We continue to have great freedom of opinion, and we also rediscover and can unite with others around the original foundation God designed. Think of how after September 11, America—and much of the world—united around the common belief that terrorism is evil. The absolutes of the Creator can unite the world in even more constructive ways.

The Costs

When we accept God's absolutes, we will also experience some disadvantages.

A loss of individual choice certainly accompanies absolutes.

When we accept God's absolutes, we accept boundaries that limit our choices. We choose not to craft our lives our own way.

We also experience *friction with our culture*, since it resists absolutes. When we propose that some absolutes apply to all of us, others perceive us as bigoted and judgmental. People get upset and afraid we might "tell them what to do." We don't fit in.

We also *struggle to identify moral absolutes*. Tim and David both come from a unity movement that stresses, "In essentials, unity; in non-essentials, liberty; and in all things, love." Sadly, while this statement refers to theological and doctrinal truth, the unity movement has, while trying to clarify the essentials, undergone numerous splits. The task of determining moral absolutes may not be any easier for us.

LIVING IT OUT

How, then, do we live with absolutes in a culture that often rejects them?

First, we must *accept absolute truth*. Remember the Barna survey we mentioned earlier that revealed only 23 percent of evangelical Christians strongly believe in absolute truth? What is God, if not absolute? Did Jesus really live and die on the cross for us? Yes, we may struggle to identify specific absolutes, but we must realize they exist and flow from God's nature and character.

We as individuals don't have the right to determine the rightness or wrongness of issues on which God has already spoken. We must accept his values. We may battle to live them out, but we cannot minimize their authority.

Second, we must *seek truth*. Dig into God's Word to

discover his boundaries! Consider how Psalm 119 encourages us to value and seek God's absolute moral values.

"The law from your mouth is more precious to me than thousands of pieces of silver and gold" (v. 72).

"Oh, how I love your law! I meditate on it all day long" (v. 97).

The truths expressed and revealed in the Bible are a guiding light for our path through life, but we must seek them and meditate on them.

Third, we must *obey truth*. The psalmist asks, "How can a young man keep his way pure? By living according to your word. I seek you with all my heart; do not let me stray from your commands" (119:9–10).

The question doesn't address only young men. All followers of Jesus must hold tightly to absolute truth. We must live what we say we believe, letting God's values direct our behavior rather than relying on our own desires or the values of our culture.

Fourth, we *flex on opinions*. Learn the difference between moral principles that guide life and casual preferences that add variety to life. And enjoy the freedom! Eating pizza and listening to good music with friends is not a moral issue. Neither is hiking in the mountains or camping on the coast. God has given us these glorious choices to enjoy within the boundaries of his moral absolutes. And we flex on the preferences of others in their musical tastes, food interests, and vacation choices.

Our culture tells us that all truth is relative, and we often slide into that belief. However, God isn't limited in his knowledge or his capacity to know. He knows what is best for his creation and has expressed those universal standards for us in his word. The rest of this book explores those values and standards more fully.

Chapter Three

Pick a Path, Any Path, to God

Pluralism Clashes with Jesus

Over 500 leaders of the 2.5 million-member Presbyterian Church (U.S.A.) gathered in 2002 to discuss the question, "Is Jesus the Savior?" A statement previously issued in 2001 by the General Assembly was ambiguous. The passionate debate produced no resolution, indicating a reluctance to acknowledge Jesus as the only Savior for all people.

President George W. Bush at the same time walked a political tightrope following the September 11, 2001, terrorist attacks. He needed, despite his own Christian faith, to affirm Muslims and include them in official ceremonies so that critics of the war on terrorism wouldn't perceive it as a war against Islam. The president's decision reinforced the prevailing view that many legitimate and equally valid paths to God exist.

Consider also the case of Carol, a university student. She felt intimidated in the classroom when her fellow students branded her a bigot because she believed Jesus to be the only way to God. Strong advocates of tolerance could not tolerate her position. After all, nobody is wrong, and nobody is right: we all perpetually seek the truth.

The philosophy of pluralism is powerfully shaping our Western culture. It insists that all faith systems have equal validity. They must, therefore, receive equal affirmation, even though they hold to different ethical teachings. Pluralism shakes our values and culture to the core. Are all religions the same? Can we pick a path, any path, to God?

CULTURE'S VALUE

What It Is

A *U.S. News & World Report* article on religion in America candidly concluded, "The problem is not that we don't believe anything but that we believe everything."[1] Most people consider pluralism to be one of our greatest virtues.

Pluralism naturally flows from the relativistic ethics that took off in the 1960s with the advent of the birth control pill, a strong anti-establishment sentiment, and widespread disillusionment with authority. As people started to set their own rules and standards, "as long as it doesn't hurt someone else," they discovered the best way to safeguard their new liberty: They could not criticize the choices of other people, since their own choices would be open to criticism. An unspoken rule developed: Don't judge anyone. This rule inevitably spilled into the realm of faith.

Any suggestion of a single way to do things or a single

faith-system that might be superior to others is now rejected in mainstream Western culture. In a letter to Dear Abby in 2002, "Happy Hindu in the Bible Belt" complained about Christian neighbors who send boxes of cookies with Christian pamphlets inside that try to subtly convert her to their faith. She concluded, "To try to convert someone to your faith implies that you consider your religious beliefs superior, and that is just plain wrong."

People who insist that Christianity is "the only way" obviously, according to our culture, lack humility, respect, and tolerance. Consequently, religious pluralism has gained popularity. Accordingly, every religious belief has equal validity, be it Hinduism, Buddhism, Islam, or Christianity. The rhetoric of "freedom of religion" means that pluralism has virtually become a Constitutional mandate.

It's for Real

Western nations once used the melting-pot analogy to describe society. In the early 1900s, sociologists falsely assumed that immigrants to the West would assimilate with the West and help forge a single new culture. Several generations proved the fallacy of this model. Today we commonly use a patchwork analogy, where each patch retains its distinctiveness but adds to the colorful whole of the culture. We don't melt together; instead we maintain our distinctives—even our religious ones—while holding together at the seams. The result? We now see mosques, synagogues, temples, and churches all in the same neighborhood. None are wrong. All are right.

The Payoffs

At the top of the list of the benefits of pluralism are *harmony and unity*. The tolerance of religious differences is neighborly and peaceable. We don't have to agree with other religious views. But if we respect them, we won't speak against them or seek to proselytize among them. Then we will all live together in peace. On the surface this makes total sense. We won't have to change. We minimize confrontation, challenge, and conflict.

Pluralism also portrays an appearance of *humility*. We appear humble when we admit we don't have an exclusive claim to truth. Anyone arrogant enough to say that others are wrong doesn't deserve an audience. We elevate humility, even that which is born out of confusion, intimidation, and ignorance. Nobody likes to be called a bigot or a know-it-all. Pluralism protects us from those labels.

Pluralism has unexpectedly reopened a door in some secular universities to reconsider the claims and evidence for Christianity. Since Christianity has become just one of many belief systems, students can evaluate it on equal terms with other values. Public discussion no longer excludes religious beliefs.

Finally, Professor Diana Eck of Harvard University, founder of "The Pluralism Project,"[2] says that people of *different faiths can learn much from each other*. Pluralism lets us learn from others and express open-mindedness. The result is a diverse network of relationships and many learning opportunities.

The Costs

Let's carefully consider the costs of pluralism. Ironically, this philosophy has failed to integrate the community into a unified whole. William Booth, of the *Washington Post*, wrote,

> Many scholars worry about the loss of community
> and shared sense of reality among Americans,
> what some call "the twilight of common dreams."
> The concern is echoed by many on both the left
> and right, and of all ethnicities, but no one seems
> to know exactly what to do about it.[3]

The philosophy of pluralism not only fails to bring unity and integration; it *contributes to the multiple fractures* clearly apparent in society. The call for tolerance, paradoxically, has become a catalyst of division.

Pluralism also *distorts the fundamental truth about God.* Benjamin Hubbard, chair of the Department of Comparative Religion at California State University, Fullerton, California, described a meeting of Jews, Christians, and Muslims, in an article for the *Los Angeles Times*. He speculated that "the God of all three faiths was weeping over global bigotry."[4] Hubbard's assumption that all three faiths worship the same God is both misguided and misguiding.

Furthermore, pluralism *undermines the confidence* that many Christians have in the biblical value system. They hold it in low esteem, since it merely expresses one option among many. They rarely read the Bible and adhere to it even less. Many experience a crisis of confidence in the Word of God.

Finally, pluralism has *introduced conflicting value systems* into

Western society. It has eroded a common base for ethical discussion and cast shadows over previously clear standards. The Bible, for example, teaches the equality of men and women, but not all religious groups share this value. In fact, some strongly deny it. In light of such fundamental differences, how can we move forward together? Minimizing such differences merely buries our heads in the sand.

GOD'S VALUE

God designed his kingdom for people from every tribe and tongue and nation with neither a Western nor an Eastern orientation. But God does not embrace pluralism. Rather, he invites all people to participate in the kingdom, based on a singular truth: Jesus Christ is Lord. The word "Lord" refers to the supremacy of Jesus: his way surpasses all others and his word takes precedence over all other teachings. Lordship is not a shared position.

What It Is

In John 14:6, Jesus said, "I am the way and the truth and the life. No one comes to the Father except through me." He claimed an exclusive position, demanding an exclusive allegiance. In the first century, critics often called Christians atheists because they refused to accept the many gods of the day. Their message that only one true God existed and that Christ Jesus is Lord proved too narrow for the ancient world, much as that seems too narrow for our world. But Christianity is not simply one option among many. As followers of Jesus, we believe he is the *only* way and the *only* hope for the world.

The early church preached "salvation is found in no one else, for there is no other name under heaven given to men by which we must be saved" (Acts 4:12). This position leaves no "wriggle room" for other faiths.

The apostle Paul similarly and adamantly proclaimed that there is only "one Lord, one faith, one baptism; and one God and Father of all" (Eph. 4:5–6). He could not accept that Jesus was one Lord among several or that the Christian faith was just one faith among many legitimate faiths. The wonder of the Gospel is that God welcomes everyone who comes, but we must come his way, not our own way. That way is Jesus Christ.

It's for Real

Jesus made it clear that we cannot walk both sides of the fence. A house divided against itself falls (see Luke 11:17). No one can serve two masters (see Matt. 6:24). The apostle Paul later asked how light and darkness can coexist (see 2 Cor. 6:14). They obviously can't. When the light comes in, the darkness goes out. What happens when you turn the lights on at home? Light and darkness cannot coexist. Neither can truth and falsehood. Any attempt to unify two mutually exclusive value systems is a fool's fantasy.

Jesus on one occasion took this principle even further. He said, "He who is not with me is against me" (Matt. 12:30). We have no neutral corner in which to quietly stand. We cannot be *for* Christ and complacently ignore what is *against* him. Christianity's defining feature claims that light and dark cannot coexist. That truth rings a death knell for pluralism.

The Payoffs

Pluralism counterfeits kingdom values. Consequently, the benefits that it *seems* to produce mirror the very benefits that the kingdom of God *does* produce. *True harmony and unity* result from a single ethical foundation. Pluralism does not resolve confrontation and conflict; it simply avoids or suppresses them. When we join together under the common umbrella of Christ as Lord, however, we share an immediate unity as the family of God. The apostle Paul wrote to the Ephesians, urging them to "keep the unity of the Spirit" (4:3) not to *create* it.

The exclusivity of Christ also makes *far greater sense* than the contradictory logic of the world. The claim of Christ to be the only way to God is either true or false. If true, then pluralism—pick a path, any path, to God—must be false. If Christ's claim is not true, then pluralism's minimal affirmation of Jesus as a great and wise teacher is wrong, and pluralism is, therefore, still false. Either way, this core cultural value proves incorrect, and the claims of Christ demonstrate more logical consistency.

The Costs

Following Christ alone involves a cost. Anytime we advocate the superiority of Christ over any other system, we can expect to hear words like "arrogant," "small-minded," "fundamentalist," "bigot," and "intolerant." These *unpleasant labels* put us in boxes that isolate us from some people. Many Christians have experienced this kind of labeling.

Personally affirming the supremacy of Christ carries major

lifestyle implications. If he alone gives abundant life, then we must follow him. If we ignore his teaching, then we reflect our ignorance, rebellion, or hypocrisy. The supremacy of Christ must change how we live.

The costs of loyalty and allegiance to Christ can be measured in terms of loss of popularity, opportunity, relationships, time, and even money. Everything in our lives comes under the scope of Christ's supremacy.

LIVING IT OUT

These first three chapters have laid a three-pillared foundation for a successful and life-changing application of kingdom principles.

The first pillar is the belief that there is a supernatural higher order that gives meaning and direction to our lives. If we choose to "leave God out of it," we will have no fallback position except our own wisdom and opinion.

The second pillar for change is realizing and agreeing that God has given certain absolutes. He can "tell us what to do" because he created us and knows what is best for us. How foolish to think that God wants to give us an abundant life but refuses to reveal the way to us. Our ethical choices must not, therefore, be determined by what others are doing or thinking but by the absolutes of God's Word.

The preceding chapter has provided the third pillar: We must choose between the vagueness of pluralism and the absolute of Christianity. Both cannot be correct. Followers of Jesus must be clear that before we learn from others, we must first test their claims against the teachings and standards of our measuring rod, Jesus Christ.

This doesn't give us permission for intolerance or antagonism. We must always treat others with respect and love. God gives us the freedom to make our choices. But we must have the conviction that not all paths lead to God and life. The path he has prescribed is the only option available.

Part Two

Attitudes Toward Others

Chapter Four

It's All About Me!

Self-Centeredness Clashes with Service

While working on this book, David and Tim met for lunch at Marie Callendar's, a restaurant known for its fine pies. Although Tim craved the boysenberry pie, he had some concerns in the weight area and declined. David, not having to worry much about his weight, pondered a slice. The waitress encouraged him to go for it. "Have some pie!" she urged. "After all, it's all about you."

Doesn't that express our culture's emphasis on self? Think of the commercials directed at pleasing yourself: "You deserve a break today"; "Have it your way"; "Who says you can't have it all?" Self-interest consumes us.

CULTURE'S VALUE

What It Is

Most of us in our Western culture care primarily about ourselves. We don't ignore others; they just come in about fourth place on our list of priorities—after "me, myself, and I." Our self-centeredness encourages us to view people as tools for advancing our interests, meeting our needs, or fulfilling our pleasures.

Andrew Carnegie, the wealthy steel industrialist, expressed the preeminence of self in his book *The Road to Business Success*:

> My advice to you, gentlemen, is to aim high. I would not give a fig to the man who does not already see himself as partner or the head of the firm. Do not rest content for a moment in your thoughts as head clerk, as foreman, or as general manager, regardless of the size of your concern, no matter how extensive. Say to yourself, "My place is at the top." Be king in your dreams.

Carnegie encouraged ambition and the advancement of self. Another advocate of living for self is William Henley, who, in the nineteenth century, penned "Invictus." It still today aptly summarizes our culture.

> Out of the night that covers me,
> Black as the Pit from pole to pole,
> I thank whatever gods may be
> For my unconquerable soul.
>
> It matters not how strait the gate,
> How charged with punishments the scroll,
> I am the master of my fate;
> I am the captain of my soul.

It's for Real

Jack Welch illustrates our culture's preoccupation with self. The retired head of General Electric, Welch brought in $1.41 million. Per month. After taxes. And what do Jack Welch's spending habits reveal about his priorities?

Newspaper reports food and beverage expenses at: $8,982. Clothing: $1,903. Country club memberships: $5,480. "Personal care": $425. Accounting, financial and tax planning: $20,000. Monthly. Now, how much did Welch give to charities? $614. Each month. Only .04 percent of his net income. What took first place in his life: self or others?

Our culture relentlessly pursues the pleasure and advancement of self. People often network in business primarily to benefit themselves, not to benefit both. Several years ago, an occasional business associate met with me (Tim) for lunch and began to praise my people skills, business sense, and how he appreciated me as a friend. But before he could set the well-baited hook, I asked if he represented a certain multi-level marketing company. He said yes, and I never heard from my admirer again.

Although some consider money as one of the greatest problems that bring stress to a marriage, many counselors view money as merely the battleground of competing selves. How shall the money be used: to benefit you or me?

Self-centeredness also invades the church. Southside Community Church came close to closing its doors. The membership continued to age, and few new members came in to replace them. Realizing that only significant changes could help reverse the decline and help the congregation reach the unchurched, the leaders changed the worship style, updated the building and programs, and implemented a system to help follow-up with visitors and members.

A stalwart of the church expressed his negative attitude toward the changes: "I like these new attendance cards you want us to fill out. I used to put money in the offering plate; now I can just put this in." His personal agenda took precedence.

Church attendees float from church to church, searching for one that meets their needs. Power struggles distract congregations. Putting out brushfires of conflict consumes resources we could otherwise direct toward our mission. One denominational study revealed that 90 percent of their churches had experienced significant friction between the pastor and elders in the previous year. Both "sides" wanted their way.

We often get involved with Christianity for our own benefit. The worship invigorates our spirit. Small group meetings provide contacts for friendships. Youth programs help our kids navigate their difficult years. And, we look forward to heaven. But these motives entrap us in self-centeredness.

We live life as we want. We use others to advance our goals. We evaluate options to discover "what's in it for me?"

The Payoffs

Indeed, self-centeredness has much in it for us. We *don't need to invest much time* in discovering the needs of others if we have little interest in meeting those needs. We have less need to delve below the surface of relationships to discover hidden troubles and needs, which in turn gives us more time for ourselves. We evaluate our options by the questions, "How will I benefit from this?" and "What will bring the best return for me?"

We live in a "get it while you can" society. And if our years on this planet are all we have, then it makes sense to please ourselves.

The Costs

The disadvantages, however, more than offset those benefits. Self-centeredness *damages relationships*. For years, Tim focused too much on his needs and not enough on those of Sheila, his wife. He didn't ignore her, but the balance was wrong and it hurt them. Mutual care is essential to meaningful relationships. Selfishness destroys loving relationships.

Self-centered behaviors often lead to *workplace battles*. People protect their turf, keeping records of one another's infractions in order to use them, if needed, as weapons. Sports fans observe the negative impact of players who care more about their personal statistics and salaries than the welfare of their team.

Last, self-centered followers of Jesus produce *ineffective churches*. Think back to Southside Community Church. The changes helped stimulate growth, bringing in new people. But some of the established members had not grown beyond their own self-centered visions. The battle continued to rage over what kind of church they would become. That uncertainty encouraged many who could have greatly helped the church to search for other church homes. The congregation could have been a light in the community, but the battle over personal preferences diminished its outreach.

GOD'S VALUE

What It Is

In contrast to self-centeredness, God calls us to serve. To care about the needs of others. To move beyond self-absorption to sacrifice. To overcome our innate selfishness.

Philippians 2:3–4 encourages us: "Do nothing out of selfish ambition or vain conceit, but in humility consider others better than yourselves. Each of you should look not only to your own interests, but also to the interests of others." Let's explore how God values service.

It's for Real

Service requires us to reject selfishness and to break the back of self-interest. To move beyond thinking primarily about ourselves.

This occurs as we balance our needs with those of other people. We don't ignore our own needs, but we lift up the needs of others as the higher priority. We craft a dual concern: our needs as well as the needs of others. We err when we move to one extreme or the other.

Tim's family left a religious group several generations ago because the group required so much sacrifice that the family's basic needs went unmet, while others lived in abundance.

How can we put the needs of others on an equal footing

with our own when it so obviously goes against our grain? We find the answer as we look at Philippians 2:5–8,

> Your attitude should be the same as that of Christ Jesus: Who, being in very nature God, did not consider equality with God something to be grasped, but made himself nothing, taking the very nature of a servant, being made in human likeness. And being found in appearance as a man, he humbled himself and became obedient to death—even death on a cross!

Jesus didn't prefer to do this. On the night before his death on the cross, he asked the Father if he had any other options. "Father, I'll do this, but isn't there another way to accomplish the same goal?" Jesus supremely demonstrated that he had not come to be served but to serve. We, like Jesus, must not live lives devoted to the pursuit of self.

When we willingly give up our needs for others, then we follow kingdom values. That's what Jesus did. Yes, we have needs. But valuing others means we sacrifice for them, just as Jesus did. Chicago Bears running back Gale Sayers defined JOY: Jesus first, Others second, and Yourself last. These kingdom values run counter to our culture.

The Payoffs

In our Philippians passage, we saw that Jesus sacrificed his own interests for the sake of others. When we do the same, we become like him. And that sacrifice transforms for us the entire Christian life in several ways.

First, we will experience *transformed relationships*. We move beyond battling one another in order to satisfy our own desires. We yearn instead to meet the needs of others. Believe us, they'll notice the difference!

Second, we will help build *effective churches*. Rather than asking, "What's in it for me?" we will give ourselves to following the leaders of our churches and to making a positive impact for God in the lives of others. Our first desire will not be to express our gifts in the pursuit of our preferences; rather, we will let our leaders identify where they need us to exercise our gifts the most. We then serve, sometimes sacrificially!

Third, we will return to *the heart of worship*—adoring God and serving him. Rather than evaluating those who lead in worship in terms of how effectively they meet *our* needs, our desire will be to connect with *God*. We will let them bring us into his presence, and we will yield our lives to him. All this is the result of an attitude of servanthood; it provides the foundation for everything worthwhile we do.

The Costs

Self-sacrifice obviously means we won't "get our way" as often. Service means letting others have their way. *We give up some things* we'd like. We may sometimes even give up our own important preferences because others have a greater need. Wives may give up their careers to serve a home and family. Husbands may give up relocating to a better job to promote family stability. Workers may give up their ideas on the best way to run the company so they can serve the team. And church members may give up their preferred style of worship to serve the efforts of the church to more effectively reach the unchurched.

LIVING IT OUT

How can we put these principles into practice?

First, let's transform our *marriages* with selfless service. Imagine the change when husbands don't expect to be served; instead, they lovingly serve their wives. Imagine the change when wives express appreciation to their husbands for that service. That's the biblical practice of mutual yielding to the needs of our mate! If we're serious about being followers of Jesus, we need to replace our self-will with God's will.

Husbands, your task comes up in Ephesians 5:25: "Husbands, love your wives, just as Christ loved the church and gave himself up for her." In the same way that Christ served the church, we husbands need to serve our wives in the big and little things. We tend to be crude, insensitive, and selfish. Ephesians 5 concludes with the command, "Each one of you also must love his wife as he loves himself" (v. 33). We husbands are to avoid selfish acts, value our spouses, and express love to them.

Wives also have a responsibility. They need to live out the value expressed by verse 22: "Wives, submit to your husbands as to the Lord." A wife should respond to her husband's loving service with support and appreciation, rather than battling to get her way.

Paul encourages husbands in this passage to meet a core need of their wives: to be loved. Wives are to meet a core need of their husbands: to be respected and appreciated. Both husbands and wives do that when they place the needs of the other above their own. Marriage then becomes a contest of grace: who can best serve the needs of the other?

Second, let's transform our *churches* with selfless service. For too long, we've battled over whose preferences for the church should take precedence. How about we allow the leaders to lead the church? Hebrews 13:17 is clear: "Obey your leaders and submit to their authority. They keep watch over you as men who must give an account. Obey them so that their work will be a joy, not a burden, for that would be of no advantage to you." The entire church benefits when its members forsake self-will.

Leaders should likewise surrender self-interest and develop a sensitivity to the needs of church members: "Be shepherds of God's flock that is under your care, *serving* as overseers—not because you must, but because you are willing, as God wants you to be; not greedy for money, but eager to *serve*; not lording it over those entrusted to you, but being examples to the flock" (1 Peter 5:2–3, emphasis added).

Third, let's transform all our *relationships* by means of selfless service. Family, work, neighborhood, church, and business connections will *all* improve when we "Do nothing out of selfish ambition or vain conceit, but in humility consider others better than yourselves" (Phil. 2:3–4).

Our culture tells us, "It's all about you." God says, "It's all about others." Let's follow God's value.

Chapter Five

I Don't Need Your Help

Independence Clashes with
Interdependence

The Declaration of Independence asserted in 1776 the rights of the thirteen colonies to independence and self-government. A very specific view of humanity, however, contributed to the birth of that document. That view is contained in the Declaration's first few lines. "We hold these truths to be self-evident, that all men are created equal, that they are endowed by their Creator with certain inalienable rights, that among these are life, liberty and the pursuit of happiness. That to secure these rights, governments are instituted among men...."

According to Jefferson and the English philosopher John Locke, who so profoundly influenced him, the job of government is to protect the rights of individuals, each of whom is equally entitled to life, liberty, and the pursuit of happiness. The Declaration focused primarily on individuals, not on communities or groups.

For over two hundred years, this issue of individual rights has steadily risen to higher and higher prominence and taken on dimensions of independence never foreseen by the founding fathers.

The lyrics sung by Frank Sinatra—"I did it my way"— have become a cultural mantra.

Should this level of self-sufficiency and autonomy surprise us? Not at all. This declaration of personal independence is the ultimate statement of personal achievement.

CULTURE'S VALUE

What It Is

Our culture idealizes rugged individualism. The cowboy who rides alone, spits tobacco, and needs only his horse provides to our culture the figure of a hero. The Lone Ranger and the Cisco Kid rode the West with partners, but had no families. They rescued the hapless, but they themselves needed no help.

We quietly esteem the tough, weather-beaten personality who declares, "I don't take no charity." We admire people who stand up for themselves and make their mark on the world. We celebrate the self-made millionaire. We grant Ph.D.s to people who produce something original. We love team sports; we also revel in individual competition. Motivational speakers urge us to take charge of our own destiny and be our own boss. "If it's going to be, it's up to me."

All of this adds up to one clear, strong message—our culture honors independence.

It's for Real

American football, basketball, and baseball may be team sports, but each player has his own contract, agent, and agenda. They may play together, but only after negotiating independent contracts. Individual music entertainers may have back-up vocalists during their performances, but few fans see the events as team productions. Many dynamic churches are identified, not by the congregation, but by a single leader —perhaps a Bill Hybels or a Rick Warren or a T. D. Jakes.

American presidents have to cooperate with Congress, but the public perceives that the president runs the country. We applaud the sacrificial efforts of the Chief Executive, or we decry his morally bankrupt policies, with little thought for the multiple layers of government staffing that comprise the clumsy apparatus of government.

Many dynamics come into play, but in this world we have to make it on our own. If we stand out, it's because we speak out for ourselves.

Now, independence possesses definite payoffs.

The Payoffs

Honor and status lead the list of benefits. The more self-made we are, the higher our reputation. We admire Bill Gates, founder of Microsoft, because he pioneered a new industry. Our culture gives kudos to independently successful people. We admire the warrior who makes a something out of nothing.

We also gain *security*. When we depend upon an employer for a salary, we become vulnerable to termination or a cutback. Self-employment and self-sufficiency avoid that weakness.

Gail Cohen, a renowned motivational speaker, says job security doesn't exist, only skill security. So our culture urges us to develop our individual skills and depend only on ourselves, the only security on which we can depend.

Another payoff is *higher productivity*. We may have learned in elementary school by experience that group projects frustrate us. Not all members do their part. Some people do poorer quality work that we have to live with. And it takes so much longer. We prefer just to do it ourselves ... to be independent. We can get more done and we do a better job.

A fourth obvious benefit is that we can *live life our way*, without accommodating the needs of others. Self-dependence reinforces our self-centeredness.

Status, security, and productivity provide strong incentives for independence. But substantial costs accompany these benefits.

The Costs

The greatest cost may be *social isolation*. The less we need people, the more isolated we become. Many CEOs drive themselves for years as independent people and finally wake up one morning beside a wife who has become a stranger.

Yerkes Observatory, associated with the University of Chicago, is the premier astrophysical laboratory in America. Donald Osterbrock's history of the institution describes the first three directors and highlights the cost of individualism.[5] History says that George Hale built the observatory; Edwin Frost let it decay; Otto Struve revived it.

However, Frost recognized the talent of Struve and nurtured the brilliant young man as his successor. Struve, on the other hand, capable as an administrator, developed a reputation for insisting that any rising stars strictly follow his lead. He did not work *with* people, but *over* them.

Osterbrock concludes, "Edwin Frost, though he may not be remembered in the annals of scientific history, was a warm, friendly person, honored and respected.... [Though] there is no Hale Street or Struve Avenue ... there are a Frost House, Frost Woods, Frost Park, Frost Drive, and Frost Circle in present-day Williams Bay.... Frost died in Billings Hospital surrounded by his wife and children; Struve, childless, died alone in a hospital in Berkeley. Which did better?" A telling question.

Social commentators observe that we live closer together but are more emotionally disconnected than ever before. We don't know how to live in community. David teaches at a Christian university and has been surprised to see how many students sit alone during the twice-weekly chapel services; 350–400 students typically attend a service, scattered throughout the 750-seat auditorium. The chapel service is a microcosm of our society.

Strangely, since we believe it's good not to *need* help, many of us become reluctant to *give* help. We expect people to be as motivated and self-sufficient as ourselves, which makes us dispassionate towards those who fail to meet our standards. Divisions and barriers grow in our relationships, further isolating us.

To be fair, our society viscerally reacts against the value of independence while, at the same time, seems to embrace it. The "team" has replaced the business CEO who barks out orders.

We're aware that collaboration is strategically important in the global village. Our culture, however, faces the simultaneous challenges of promoting both rugged individualism as well as collaboration. Contradictory values compete, which leads to ethical confusion.

GOD'S VALUE

What It Is

God's countercultural value is interdependence. In his kingdom, we really do need each other. The late German theologian Karl Barth once delivered a series of lectures in which he consistently and correctly replaced the word "church" with "community." Jesus didn't envision a kingdom of loners but an interdependent community of believers who would support each other and achieve more together than they ever could alone. Such a community develops interconnectedness and interdependence.

We must be careful not to confuse individuality with individualism. Individuality celebrates individual differences. God has created each of us with unique gifts, abilities, and strengths that make up the mosaic of life. Individualism, however, decides that we can have our way without regard or need for others. That isolationist attitude does not belong in God's kingdom.

It's for Real

When in ancient Israel times got tough and poverty flourished, the simplest philosophy would have been, "every one for themselves." But God gave specific instructions for the community to care for the widows, orphans, and strangers in the land. Those with resources were to help those in need. Nobody stood alone; everyone was connected. Therefore, when Achan sinned (see Josh. 7:22–26), his whole family was punished with him. Interdependence and interconnectedness characterized God's people.

Jesus taught his disciples centuries later not to freelance but to serve. They would receive support from others, give support to each other, and model a higher love for each other than for themselves (see John 13:34–35).

The apostle Paul in the first decades of the church described that community was the body of Christ in which different people had different functions but each was equally important (see 1 Cor. 12:14–26). Paul provided a powerful image of the kingdom community—the ear that needs the eye that needs the foot.

The apostle James later wrote, "Is anyone of you sick? He should call he elders of the church ..." (James 5:14). Call for the elders? The independent spirit of today arm wrestles with this concept. We ride it out. We don't want to bother people. We handle it alone or share it only with the family. But involve others in my need? No way! We don't want to be in anyone's debt. But James prescribes interdependence; it presumes life in community: receiving on one occasion but giving on the next.

The kingdom of God consists of people who realize their desperate need to connect with someone—Jesus Christ. We who populate the kingdom of God are not self-made. Neither are we self-sufficient. We depend upon the work of God's Holy Spirit to accomplish every good work within us. He transforms our own lives and blesses the lives of others. It makes no sense, therefore, to enter the kingdom in utter dependence and then choose to live independently.

The Payoffs

We frequently hear the buzz word "*synergy*," which simply means that we achieve more together than individually. David and Tim have learned that in this book! Collaboration allows us to bounce ideas off each other and to sharpen each other's thinking and writing. This synergy happens all the time in the corporate world as businesses merge to achieve more profit together than they can alone. In 2001, Time Inc. established a partnership with America Online. AOL promoted Time Inc. magazines online and generated 1.5 million subscriptions in 2001—about 100,000 a month. Meanwhile, Time distributed AOL discs with its magazines and generated about 67,000 new AOL registrations per month. Good marketing? Absolutely! But even more, interdependence.

Enhanced relationships also result. Our cultural values tend to isolate us from each other, but God's values reconnect us. Interdependence helps us discover new levels of relationship. Meaningful relationships, not money or toys, provide the richest lives. The two-way traffic of receiving and giving nurtures those friendships. When we only *take* from someone, we become a project, not a friend. When we only *give* to someone, we become a benefactor, not a friend. Rich relationships engage us in both giving and receiving. The accountability relationships advocated by such groups as Promise Keepers provide a good example of how interdependence bonds people together.

Finally, interdependence provides a marvelous *antidote to the selfishness* our culture fosters. Tim would have loved to have all of his ideas incorporated into this book. Even though Tim viewed his ideas as the best, David sometimes disagreed! But the interdependence of writing balanced Tim's innate tendency toward selfishness. "I've learned that working with David has forced me to consider others more, to listen more carefully to their ideas. That's touched other areas of my life as well."

But trade-offs exist. Any time we change a core value, it will change the way we live, and that will mean upheaval and costs.

The Costs

Interdependence *consumes time*. Tasks take longer to complete. We have to contact people we've previously ignored. We need to send emails and add to our address books people we have previously considered "marginal." We find ourselves helping to fix a car, repair a washing machine, mend a dress, or prepare a meal for someone else. All this builds a foundation for true community—sharing our lives with each other.

Our pride also takes a hit. Some of us choose independence so we can remain aloof. Interdependence shakes the bottom out of this. We cannot depend on someone else while we also regard ourselves as superior to them. Interdependence humbles us; we recognize that we exist as one *of* many, not one *apart from* many.

Our wallet also feels the brunt of this kingdom value. As we engage in genuine community and enter into each other's lives more fully and more enthusiastically, *hidden financial costs emerge*. We will want to support those who are hurting, give to those who are without, and uphold those in crisis. That may include flowers, chocolates, payment of utility bills, cards that express appreciation, scholarships, food, and long-distance phone calls.

Yes, we need to consider a broad range of costs—but the benefits far outweigh the price we pay!

LIVING IT OUT

A commitment to interdependence deeply affects us, especially when we realize that in true communities we don't always get to pick and choose those with whom we connect.

As a young church-planter in Western Australia, David had to deal with some diverse personalities. For the first time, he learned that difficult people play an important role in our lives. If no one ever rubs us the wrong way, through whom will we learn patience? If nobody offends us, how will we learn forgiveness? If we are indeed to grow in the fruit of the Spirit, we really do need others—the easy, the difficult, the kind, and the abrasive others. And they need us. God's strategy to shape us involves others.

Interdependence means listening more to each other, especially in our families. Too many marriages merely coexist; too many families just share a roof. When we are too busy to listen, we are too busy to build relationships and, therefore, too busy to practice interdependence. Listening leads us in the right direction.

In our churches and small groups, interdependence may mean a higher level of active listening that requires mutual honesty and openness. We will need to observe others' needs, but we will also need to express our own needs. An "I'm OK" attitude may be legitimate at times—when things *are* OK. This can, however, become a habit of the heart that seeks status in the eyes of the group and safety from the pain others might inflict on us. Openness, though risky, provides the foundation of true community.

Interdependence in the workplace may require delegation of responsibilities, trusting coworkers more, listening to coworkers or employees more, and devoting ourselves to intentional team-building. Interdependence turns hierarchies into collaborative structures.

When Tim was in his twenties, he found paradise. God provided a job caretaking an unused guest ranch in the mountains above Taos, New Mexico. Hiking, trout fishing, and the glory of nature were everywhere. An introvert and nature lover, he vowed never to leave. After two years of growth, though, he realized that living in the mountains isolated him from the people God meant him to be involved with.

He entered vocational ministry and had opportunities to touch and be touched by other lives. As great as Taos was, he found something greater. Community.

Consider this portion of Martin Luther King Jr.'s famous "I have a dream" speech, delivered on the steps at the Lincoln

Memorial in Washington, D.C., on August 28, 1963:

> The marvelous new militancy which has engulfed
> the Negro community must not lead us to distrust
> of all white people, for many of our white brothers,
> as evidenced by their presence here today, have
> come to realize that their destiny is tied up with our
> destiny and their freedom is inextricably bound to
> our freedom. We cannot walk alone.

It's true. We cannot walk alone.

Chapter Six

Winning Isn't Everything; It's the Only Thing

Competition Clashes with Cooperation

To the surprise of everyone, in 1980 amateur runner Rosie Ruiz won the women's race of the eighty-fourth Boston Marathon. Suspicions arose the next day, however, when Ruiz didn't appear in race videotapes until the end of the event. Officials theorized that Ruiz hopped on a subway for much of the race, ran the final mile or half-mile, and then proudly accepted the winner's medal. Although she never admitted to cheating, officials disqualified her.

Meanwhile, on the other side of the world there lived Jim—a warm, friendly, easygoing, family man. Few people welcomed him on jobsites in western Australia. He tested concrete to make sure that the pressure of competition didn't result in concrete suppliers compromising quality standards.

In a recent television drama, one of the characters had been undermining a coworker's marriage and personal life to get his job. When her boss confronted her about it, she denied doing anything inappropriate and defended her underhanded actions as "career enhancement." In a dog-eat-dog world, she shamelessly pressed a competitive edge.

Maybe Lucy was right when she told Charlie Brown, "Winning isn't everything; but losing is nothing!" She certainly expressed a common cultural attitude. "Winning isn't everything; it's the only thing!" "No one remembers who comes in second." "All's fair in love and war." "Win at all costs." That attitude reflects something our culture highly values—competition.

CULTURE'S VALUE

What It Is

The *Random House Dictionary* provides two synonyms for competition: "struggle" and "rivalry." We compete for money, for glory, for affection, and for acceptance. We play for fun, but we compete for something else.

It's for Real

Competition grips our culture. Competitive sports have become a multi-billion dollar industry. Businesses compete aggressively for the customer's dollars. Students compete for grades and scholarships. Politicians compete for votes. Television stations compete for viewers. We even compete for marriage partners! The popular television series *Survivor* is a sound bite from our culture. Participants vie with each other to be the last remaining contestant—the survivor—thereby winning the cash. A competitive spirit grips our culture. Every ad we see, every salesperson who calls, and every effort we make to win, reveals the strength of this core value.

The Payoffs

Competition obviously brings advantages.

It produces *excellence*. Charles Darwin called it "survival of the fittest." Only the best make it through to the next round of life. This process eventually creates a superior product, superior student, superior politician. The drive to win makes us work harder and better. Standards often rise with competition.

Competition also enhances *self-worth*. Most people like a winner, and those of us who emerge victorious in the struggle feel good about ourselves. We even become ambitious for greater victories, believing in ourselves in new ways. Self-image strengthens when we win.

Competition helps us *reach our potential*. If we might otherwise settle for mediocrity, a competitive environment motivates and inspires us. Competition brings out the best in us and drives us beyond what we previously thought possible.

Yes, competition carries some definite advantages. But a downside exists.

The Costs

Competition *hurts the loser*. Competition, by its very nature, creates a win-lose scenario. Somebody wins. Somebody loses. The winner often wins at the expense of the loser. Consider gambling. Two people (or a person and a machine) compete for each other's money. One of the two will win, but at the expense of the other. The winner is richer and the loser is poorer.

Don't expect a win-lose scenario to benefit relationships. A husband and wife, or even just two good friends, may compete to win an argument. Is winning healthy, especially when the contest merely continues to the next occasion? Stephen R. Covey noted in 7 *Habits of Highly Effective People* that people who have healthy relationships usually seek a win-win outcome, not a win-lose one. Win-win situations, interestingly, are noncompetitive at heart.

Competition can *undermine such important values* as honesty, integrity, and compassion. Recall Rosie Ruiz, Jim, and the TV character, whom we cited earlier. Competition in each case undermined integrity or compassion.

Vivian Paley has written books about children and their moral and social development. She sees competition as the serpent in our children's gardens. She believes that children all start their education with the highest morality of all, but the competitive demands of "Be smart," "Be fast," "Know more than someone else does" quickly erode their morality. A lifestyle of compromised values results.

Finally, competition can become *a way of life that isolates us*. Years ago, David played squash—the English sport from which American racquetball developed. Over time, he became quite proficient at it. His good friend Peter, however, had never played the sport and he wanted to learn. They went out onto the court together and, rather than just volley back and forth, they competed. David's experience clearly gave him an advantage over Peter. Game after game, David demolished him. David felt good about himself. Peter felt demoralized.

They never played squash again. They remain friends, but the aggressively competitive experience isolated them from being able to play that sport with each other again.

So, in the counter-culture of the kingdom, what place does competition have? Or, more constructively, what countervalue does God provide?

GOD'S VALUE

What It Is

Stories of competition fill the Bible. Not surprisingly, they often feature destructive endings. The first such story has its setting in the Garden of Eden.

Adam and Eve have rebelled against God. He then pronounces a curse on Eve. "Your *desire* will be for your husband, and he shall rule over you" (Gen. 3:16, emphasis added). Although the first part sounds like a blessing to the husband, it actually summarizes the curse. The word *desire* next occurs in the following chapter where the Lord says to Cain that "sin is crouching at your door; it *desires* to have you, but you must master it" (4:7).

Rather than the affectionate desire that men would want, this is a competitive, dominating attitude. Adam had, just prior to God's pronouncement, turned on Eve and blamed her for their predicament. Ever had that happen to you? You didn't feel warmth and affection, but anger and competition. That makes the second half of the curse sensible. Eve will want to get the better of her husband, but his sheer physical strength means that he will rule over her. Their relationship, once marked by thoughtful cooperation, becomes competitive and unhealthy.

Then, immediately after the Lord finished speaking, Adam did a strange thing. "[Straight away] the man called his wife's name Eve" (3:20). In the Bible, when someone gives a name, they have power and authority over that which they named. Adam's actions confirm the new competitive environment. He named his wife to claim power over her.

The kingdom of God, however, reverses the effects of the Fall and restores creation to the perfect order God intended. In short, we replace competition with the kingdom value of cooperation.

It's for Real

Although Jesus was walking with them in Mark 9, his disciples thought he couldn't hear them, and they argued about who was the greatest. How outrageous—raw competition at its ugliest. Politics and preferences threatened this little band of believers in the same way it still threatens bands of believers. Jesus later sat down with them and asked, "What were you talking about as we walked here?" None of them wanted to admit to the crass competitive spirit that had infected them.

So Jesus said, "If any one wants to be first, he shall be last of all and servant of all."

God cares more about service than about competition. He doesn't want us to compete for fame, recognition, or glory. He wants us to work *with* others, not to climb *over* or bulldoze *through* them. We need hearts that cooperate rather than compete.

Jesus, in order to reinforce this principle, took a little child and told his followers to become like little children. Better to be the lowliest members of society than proudly to compete for honor.

Of course, the New Testament writers grasped this truth. They consistently wrote that the new community of believers should be marked by a series of "one anothers": love one another, forgive one another, be subject to one another, defer to one another, pray for one another, admonish one another, encourage one another. Such words stand in stark contrast to the notion of "compete with one another."

The Payoffs

When we choose to live by the principle of cooperation rather than competition, several benefits emerge.

First, our *relationships change for the better.* When we abandon competition, we become free to want the best for others. We can only break beyond superficial levels of relationships when we cooperate and serve, rather than compete.

Second, when our relationships improve, they impact the entire community. Imagine a community where people implicitly trust each other because they don't compete with each other.

Finally, *life itself becomes more enjoyable.* As we commit ourselves to cooperation, we encounter less stress. Many of the daily pressures that we face—in our relationships, work, churches, and schools—spring from a competitive approach to life. Although this may sound both difficult and idealistic, it is doable.

If we choose, however, to embrace this countercultural value, it will cost us.

The Costs

First, our pursuit of excellence requires us genuinely to do all things as "to the Lord" (Col. 3:23). That will require *a difficult shift of focus*. Some of us, without competition to drive us, tend to be lazy. As believers, though, we are always to strive for excellence, to honor our excellent God. One cost will be the need to adopt this new motivation for excellence—"Do all things as unto the Lord."

Second, some of our *friends simply won't understand*. They may accuse us of lacking the "killer instinct." Lets face it: *Killer* and *cooperation* don't usually find themselves in the same sentence. We may not be as welcome in circles driven by a dominant competitive spirit.

Third, we might have to reconsider how we do business, how we play sports, how we function at the university, and especially how we relate to others in our church. We may have to make some *major changes in habits, policies, and practices*.

Fourth, and perhaps most difficult of all, *we won't always get our way*. Ouch. That hurts. We've grown accustomed to having our way, preserving our rights, and doing whatever we like. Cooperation means we will become more devoted to working with each other for the common good of others rather than competing with each other for our own individual good. Don't be deluded; this countercultural value is expensive. But look again at the payoffs.

LIVING IT OUT

So what does this mean for our day-to-day life? If we take cooperation seriously, it will mean substantial changes.

When David embraces God's value of cooperation, his marriage will change. He and his wife, Kim, have occasional marital disputes. The issue sometimes disappears in a fog of competitive responses. Both partners maintain that they are the less appreciated party. Both partners insist that they work harder and deserve more affirmation. We've all been there and keep revisiting that place. But what a difference takes place when we choose to cooperate rather than compete. No longer do we need to surpass our partner. Rather, we stop to listen and to understand each other, to appreciate one another's unique perspectives. That allows us to work with each other to address the issue rather than to run roughshod over each other.

When Tim embraces the kingdom value of cooperation, he doesn't compare his student evaluations to other professors' ratings as a means of validating himself as a teacher. Rather, he rejoices that God has given him the privilege of joining other professors in shaping the lives of students to better serve Christ.

Competition lacks grace. Cooperation oozes it. In relationships, when we have to win, no one really does.

What choices do we make day-by-day? Our culture urges us to compete and to win. But the counter-culture of our faith calls us to live differently—embracing cooperation and discarding competition. It's revolutionary and it's not easy. But it will dramatically change and enrich our lives.

Chapter Seven

Just Do It!

Sexual Freedom Clashes with Purity

He couldn't resist the opportunities. He had led the Lakers to five world championships in basketball. Yet, while still in his prime at only 32 years old, Magic Johnson announced his retirement. He'd contracted HIV, the virus that leads to AIDS (Acquired ImmunoDeficiency Syndrome). Sexual promiscuity bore a heavy price tag for the Magic man.

Sex saturates our culture. Newspapers, magazines, television, and bumper stickers all promote it. Sexual innuendos are everywhere. We can listen to explicit discussions on the radio and have sex over the phone. A whirlpool of pornographic materials swirls on the internet ready to suck us in. Sex-shops, strip clubs, and XXX theaters thrive within a short drive. Sex fills tabloids, music, and novels. The media dispenses it like we add spice to our food.

Many young kids no longer have to experiment with sex.

They are experts. Recent surveys indicate that in Britain 25 percent of girls and 34 percent of boys under the age of sixteen are sexually experienced.[6] In the USA, 34 percent of high school sophomores have had sex, and that number rises to 60 percent by the twelfth grade.[7] Sixteen percent of high school sophomores have had four or more sexual partners.[8]

CULTURE'S VALUE

What It Is

This preoccupation with sexuality grew out of the sexual revolution of the 1960s. We called it "free love." The term alluded to freedom from social restraints, inhibitions, guilt, shame, and responsibility. We eliminated the dominant moral value that linked sexual activity to marriage. We approved of almost any behavior between consenting adults. Our culture glories in sexual freedom.

It's for Real

Consider one of the most prominent examples of our day. Former President Clinton was impeached in 2000 for lying to Congress over his sexual relationship with White House intern Monica Lewinsky.

Although he first denied that anything occurred between Ms. Lewinsky and him, overwhelming evidence emerged to the contrary. Clinton then defended himself with two arguments. He denied that the liaison with Lewinsky was an act of sex. Next, he claimed that mutual consent made it acceptable. For most people and Congress, the outrage centered on the president's lying and evasion, not his adultery. Few people cared that a married man committed adultery. Lying to Congress was unconscionable; adultery seemed OK. Many believed that illicit sexual choices don't impact a person's capacity to lead the nation.

The same standards serve the rest of the nation. We don't restrain our sexual encounters by boundaries of decency, marriage, or love. If it involves two consenting adults, it's OK, and that goes for homosexual acts as well. The voice of restraint has become little more than a whisper. Debra Haffner, in her book *Beyond the Big Talk*, proposes five criteria for a "moral sexual relationship:" that it be consensual, non-exploitative, honest, mutually pleasurable, and protected against disease and pregnancy. Love, exclusive relationship, commitment, and marriage no longer fit into our secular culture's assessment of morality.

Western culture glories in its sexual freedom.

The Payoffs

Sexual freedom involves a *"try before you buy"* philosophy, suggesting that sex without commitment will help us decide about commitment. This "sampling experience"—pleasurable, casual, and without obligation—sounds attractive.

For some, sex *satisfies* seemingly irresistible hormonal impulses and results in the relief of sexual tension. The philanderer and the rapist both seek this release.

For others, the psychological issue trumps the biological. They want the *conquest*, the thrill of the chase. They feel powerful. Many marriages collapse at this point. Once the conquest is complete, the thrill diminishes. Let's move to the next challenge.

For still others, sex serves as a tool for *survival or advancement.* It opens doors to acquire money, gifts, influence, or affluence. Women have often used their sexual attraction toward this end.

Finally, still others advocate sexual freedom to quiet an uneasy conscience. We don't like sexual *exploitation* but accept sexual *experimentation.* We don't honor sexual abuse, even though we reluctantly concede its practice. And we admire the artistry of the successful seducer. Sexual freedom allows us to appeal to a majority practice in order to justify our base desires and soften any guilt we may sense.

The Costs

Sexual freedom, nevertheless, is costly.

The *loss of human dignity* tops the list. When we see people as mere objects of our sexual desires, we diminish their dignity and their humanity. It results in abuse, emotional detachment, and aggression. Think carefully about these three terms. They describe the pornography industry. The rise of child sex abuse, date rape, and failed marriages all occur when sex becomes an end in itself.

Years ago, Hugh Hefner, founder of the Playboy empire, was asked on a television program when his own daughter was going to come out dressed as a bunny "to join the party." The usually unflappable Hefner hesitated and answered that his daughter would work as an administrator in the company, not a model. Christian recording artist Barry McGuire later exposed

Hefner's hypocrisy by writing a song with the blunt lyrics, "You want to do to other men's daughters what you don't want them to do to your own."

Tragically, the "free love" movement has catapulted our culture way beyond Hefner's hesitation. Far too many men will now do to their own daughters what they would do to others if given the opportunity. We fail to preserve human dignity and to value sex as something sacred even within our own families.

This age of sexual freedom has produced an *endless trail of broken marriages*. Dr. Colin Wilson, England's first "Dr. Sex" in the early 1970s, notes, "Fifty years ago, for most people, marriage was where your sex life began. Today, for many people, it's where it ends." Few among us expect people to reserve themselves for a single partner when we live in a culture that downplays commitment and loyalty and faithfulness. Indeed, many middle-aged men like to boast about their "trophies," referring to mistresses with whom they maintain extra-marital affairs that help them feel virile and alive. But such sexual license betrays and sabotages the trust on which a meaningful marriage depends.

Recent studies reveal that the divorce rate increases 50 percent for couples who live together before marriage. Other research indicates that sexual satisfaction and frequency among married couples exceeds that for single persons. When we abandon purity, we lose the very thing we seek—fulfillment.

Perhaps the most significant cost, however, is *spiritual*.

We've reduced sex to a purely physical act, like eating, sleeping, and jogging. This reduction ignores the spiritual realities associated with human sexuality. The sexual freedom we embrace creates a spiritual wilderness.

GOD'S VALUE

What It Is

God counters the cultural value with purity. Not prudery, purity. God doesn't call us to be self-righteous prigs when it comes to sex. He does, however, call us to holiness, to live with sensitivity to the sacred.

Purity does not necessitate a lifetime of chastity. God does not require us to deny our sexuality or avoid sexual experiences altogether. But purity and holiness mean we practice our sexuality within godly boundaries rather than as our culture propounds. The boundary is not perpetual abstinence but responsible and committed relationships.

It's for Real

God originally created us as sexual beings with a desire for intimacy. The Lord told Adam and Eve in Genesis 1:28 (NKJV) to "be fruitful and multiply." He not only gave the instructions but all the drive and equipment necessary to do so. He also provided a context—an exclusive, permanent commitment between a man and a woman.

Look at the blueprint the Bible provides:

> For this reason a man shall leave his father and his
> mother, and shall be joined to his wife; and they

shall become one flesh. And the man and his wife
were both naked and were not ashamed (Gen.
2:24–25 NASB).

Three key concepts leap out of this text with a significant
order. Sexual fulfillment means becoming "one flesh" with
someone else. No shame, no embarrassment, no guilt. But that
fulfillment has two important prerequisites. We can summarize
them with two words: "exclusive" and "permanent."

The biblical writer talks first about *leaving* father and
mother. That means leaving behind the most treasured and
significant relationships of the past to forge a new and exclusive
relationship. He then adds a second element to the blueprint:
the archaic word *cleave*. It means "to hang on tightly and never
let go." Not a casual *touch* but a permanent *grip*. Only with these
two preconditions in place can two people truly become one
flesh. The sexual encounter takes on a whole new dimension.
Post-it note relationships, where we stick just briefly, are not the
biblical context for sexual expression. As with most biblical
teaching, secular Western culture has reversed this process.
People often hope that casual sexual encounters will result in
something permanent. It seldom happens because that order
reverses the designer's intent. And sexual expression outside
God's blueprint brings destruction.

That's why sexual purity is so fundamental. God does not seek
to rain on our parade. Just the opposite. He wants the absolute
best for us. Sexual purity provides that. Immorality does not.

The values of the kingdom once again run counter to the
values of society. Society talks about consent, non-exploitation,

honesty, mutual pleasure, and safety. But God built these very things into marriages marked by exclusivity (leaving) and permanence (cleaving). In a strange way, our culture is moving back toward the biblical norm but still resists the notion of exclusive commitment.

The New Testament provides frequent reinforcement for teachings about sexual purity.

> God wants you to live a pure life. Keep yourselves from sexual promiscuity. Learn to appreciate and give dignity to your body, not abusing it, as is so common among those who know nothing of God (1 Thess. 4:3–5 MSG).

> Honor marriage, and guard the sacredness of sexual intimacy between wife and husband. God draws a firm line against casual and illicit sex (Heb. 13:4 MSG).

The Payoffs

When we do it God's way, *sex becomes satisfying.* When love and commitment undergird sex, rather than lust and exploitation, it takes on powerful dimensions. Sex then *builds* rather than *destroys.* Sex produces *bonding* rather than *bondage.* Sex *enriches* relationships instead of undermining them. Sex springs out of *security* rather than *insecurity,* and it is *selfless* rather than *self-serving.* And this leads us to fullness of life: God's way.

Purity affirms the conviction that God designed sex exclusively for marriage. It also *strengthens our spiritual connection* with each other and with God. The Bible tells us our bodies are temples of the Holy Spirit and we are not our own. When we avoid immorality, we glorify God with our bodies (see 1 Cor. 6:18–20). Sex has spiritual ramifications far beyond the biological.

Purity also *restores human dignity.* The degradation in the pornography industry destroys human dignity; purity affirms it. As we strip off clothing, we strip away human dignity, and we undermine the very value of human life. It is no coincidence that we see today's sexual freedom matched by a callous disregard for unborn life (abortion) and low-quality life (euthanasia). When we respect human dignity, we respect human life. When we value purity, we value life itself.

Finally, purity *produces wholesome relationships.* Purity builds trust. Impurity destroys it. Purity respects people. Impurity respects performance. When we see people as human beings made in the image of God rather than as human machines made to satisfy our sex drive, we can cultivate wholesome relationships. Otherwise we see each other as commodities and products that we use and discard.

The Costs

Abstinence may seem costly because restraint from intimacy can produce *loneliness.* After all, God created us for intimacy. At such times, we can feel isolated and frustrated. For this very reason, meaningful nonsexual friendships and a walk with God become indispensable.

Mounting peer pressure levies another cost. Our desire to fit in with the group makes choosing purity very difficult. Others won't applaud such a choice. Some groups will not welcome us when we embrace such values. As the Bible says, light dispels darkness. And when people choose to live in the dark, then light becomes an unwelcome intrusion.

Finally, the choice for purity affects the places we go, the things we watch and listen to, and the material we read. Rather than just *adding* purity to our lives, it becomes a pervasive value that changes how we live.

LIVING IT OUT

When we choose purity, we swim against the culture's tide. Tim remembers that as a teen he tried to get as close to impurity as he could while remaining pure. Quite a contradiction! Let's commit to intentionally move as far from impurity as we can. Since sex permeates our culture, we need to examine prayerfully how we might minimize our exposure. Let's identify what tempts us and avoid that as best we can.

How will that look? Some of us will need to be much more discretionary about what we allow to pour into our homes through cable television and the internet. We may even need accountability partners. David's family—he has three young sons—chose to place the home computer in the kitchen because it's an easy location to monitor what comes through the modem.

We might consider other practical steps. We may need to eliminate some magazines, delete some email jokes instead of reading and forwarding them, modify or end some unhealthy relationships. Most strategically, let's bring the topics of sexual freedom and purity into the open and discuss them seriously, especially within the family setting.

Chapter Eight

Whatever Makes You Happy

Tolerance Clashes with Tough Love

Nestled in a medium-sized community in central California's coastal hills, Grace Church had been for its entire forty years a comfortable place to worship. People enjoyed one another, and while the congregation never grew much, it also never struggled much. A passing comment destroyed the carefully crafted tranquility.

One of the church leaders had lunch with a new business associate. The associate couldn't hide his amazement when he learned that his friend attended Grace Church. "You mean, you go to that church that allows adulterers to teach Sunday school?"

Everyone in town apparently knew about Dean's numerous affairs, except his church and his wife. The elders, having never previously confronted such a situation, studied the Bible, then called Dean in to ask him about the charges. Dean acknowledged their accuracy but then led a fight against the elders.

"What I do on my own is my business. You have no right to interfere."

Surprisingly, many church members agreed with Dean. They tolerated his behavior, believing that whatever private behavior makes a person happy is his own business. Twenty people eventually left the church along with Dean. They thought that the church judged Dean in a critical manner and didn't express love and grace to him.

Their community divided over the definition of tolerance. What behavior ought we tolerate? Should we, ever, infringe on another person's right to do as he or she pleases?

CULTURE'S VALUE

What It Is

The *Cambridge International Dictionary of English* defines tolerance as "willingness to accept behavior and beliefs which are different from your own, although you might not agree with or approve of them."

The mainstream postmodern world considers tolerance the only absolute by which society must live. It urges us to accept all cultures, all races, all sexual preferences, all socioeconomic classes, all religions, and all people. Tolerance has become *the* unifying social principle.

It's for Real

Tolerance in our society covers a wide range. At one end, we find the benevolent libertarian belief that "each person has the right to live his life in any way he chooses so long as he respects the equal rights of others," as expressed by David Boaz in *Libertarianism*. At the other extreme, groups such as NAMBLA, the North American Man-Boy Love Association, believe that we should not only tolerate but encourage sexual behavior between men and boys under the age of eight years.

"Live and let live" is the mantra of our culture. It expresses tolerance, as does our chapter title, "Whatever makes you happy." Tolerance is the dominant ethical value of our culture today.

The Payoffs

Tolerance, of course, yields lots of benefits. First, we link tolerance with *freedom*. Tim loves riding his motorcycle and on occasion would willingly sacrifice a bit of safety to experience the wind blowing through his remaining hair. The laws of California, however, won't tolerate that. He would appreciate a little more tolerance!

Second, tolerance affirms the *worth of the individual*. If people openly disagree with us or argue with us, we may feel threatened or undervalued. We, therefore, affirm each other by not disputing others' views. Have you ever noticed that even in Bible study groups people are never wrong? They just hold *interesting* or *diverse* views. Similarly, in many households, parents never correct or rebuke their children lest the children feel devalued. Tolerance makes us feel good.

Finally, tolerance *decreases judgmentalism* and elevates the way others view us. We don't look down on others as much, even when we disapprove of their behavior. Others also think more highly of us. Relationships seem to improve when we eliminate such moral judgments. Tolerance thus appears to be a "win-win" for all of us. We feel so much better about ourselves and experience much less conflict.

The Costs

The advantages of tolerance, however, dissipate when we push it to an extreme. Let's consider two categories.

Within the family of faith, an attitude of tolerance will encourage us to ignore *destructive behavior*. The first century church in Corinth exulted in their tolerance. "It is actually reported that there is sexual immorality among you, and of a kind that does not occur even among pagans: A man has his father's wife. And you are proud! Shouldn't you rather have been filled with grief … ?" (1 Cor. 5:1–2).

The Corinthian church, much like some in Grace Church, took pride in their tolerance. Rather than reacting to sin with grief, they responded with pride.

Second, in the name of tolerance, we sometimes accept behavior that hurts society. Should we tolerate NAMBLA when we see the damage their behavior brings to young boys? As our culture debates the legitimacy of homosexual marriage, we need to recognize its destructive potential for families and society.

We pay a price for tolerance when we accept damaging beliefs and behaviors.

GOD'S VALUE

What It Is

In place of unrestricted tolerance, God expects us to value tough love. A love for other people that is deep enough to risk intervening in their business. A love that doesn't control others but stands with them to help them avoid damaging choices. A love with accountability. This accountability touches two areas.

First, tough love flows between Christians when we care enough about the person to be involved with them despite the risks.

Second, we need to love the culture and its people enough to take a stand against actions and attitudes that become destructive.

It's for Real

Tough love means we act in the best interests of the person we love. Think about these verses from 1 Corinthians 13:

> Love is patient, love is kind. It does not envy, it does not boast, it is not proud. It is not rude, it is not self-seeking, it is not easily angered, it keeps no record of wrongs. Love does not delight in evil but rejoices with the truth. It always protects, always trusts, always hopes, always perseveres (13:4–7).

Can we possibly love others, see danger coming their way, and ignore it, saying, "Whatever makes you happy?" Yes, they bear the responsibility for their choices, but our love for them requires that we make them aware of it and turn them away from danger.

Tough love rests on two principles. First, individuals bear the responsibility for their actions. "Each one should test his own actions. Then he can take pride in himself, without comparing himself to somebody else, for each one should carry his own load" (Gal. 6:4–5). God grants each person the right to make decisions as well as to face the consequences. We bear our own load; we can't blame others for our choices.

Second, love demands mutual accountability. The Galatians passage commands us, "Brothers, if someone is caught in a sin, you who are spiritual should restore him gently. But watch yourself, or you also may be tempted. Carry each other's burdens, and in this way you will fulfill the law of Christ" (6:1–2).

We don't remove their load, only the burden beyond what they can bear. We sometimes provide a broader perspective; we may at other times stand shoulder-to-shoulder with them to deal with the issue. We have a responsibility not to allow fellow followers of Jesus to go their own way regardless of the resulting damage. Individuals can reject what we offer, but we need to act lovingly toward them. That sometimes, oftentimes, requires tough love.

The Payoffs

The greatest benefit of tough love may be that it fosters more love. The more we act lovingly toward one another, the more love flourishes in the world. Tolerance may simply be the result of laziness or fear or serving self. When we practice tough love, or what some call "carefrontation," everyone benefits.

Tough love also enhances our Christian witness. "By this all men will know that you are my disciples, if you love one another" (John 13:35). When we lovingly confront one another, love grows. People can see our active concern for one another. And love that actively strives for the best on someone's behalf always seems more attractive than the indifference of tolerance.

Tough love also increases purity. Many of us have blind spots—sin areas we can't see. When others point them out to us, we then gain the ability to become more Christlike. We may even be aware of the weakness but don't think it's important, or that we can on our own overcome it. When others lovingly involve themselves in the process, we increase motivation and gain spiritual strength from that cooperative action.

The Costs

When we address problems in others, however, we may seem intrusive. Sticking our noses in other people's business doesn't usually produce appreciation. Many in Grace Church were offended that the church leaders meddled in Dean's private life. They thought only Dean and his wife needed to be involved and that the church was almost cultlike in its attempts to control them.

We also have to fight the tendency to become critical and begin too closely to scrutinize people's private business. We can easily go to extremes and move beyond love into judgmentalism. Tough love doesn't gather information for a gossip column but nurtures and supports others.

Finally, tough love can fail to extend grace. It can slip into legalism when we see ourselves as the moral police of the community. It's important that legalism does *not* become an element of tough love. We all are sinners in need of grace, bearing each other's burdens.

LIVING IT OUT

The church in Corinth struggled to practice tough love. They proudly tolerated a man involved sexually with his stepmother. What was Paul's advice to them?

> And you are proud! Shouldn't you rather have
> been filled with grief and have put out of your
> fellowship the man who did this? Even though I
> am not physically present, I am with you in spirit.
> And I have already passed judgment on the one
> who did this, just as if I were present. When you
> are assembled in the name of our Lord Jesus and I
> am with you in spirit, and the power of our Lord
> Jesus is present, hand this man over to Satan, so
> that the sinful nature may be destroyed and his
> spirit saved on the day of the Lord (1 Cor. 5:2–5).

Paul commanded them to confront the man, and if he was unwilling to change, to put him out of the church. Keep in mind, though, this process has two purposes: first, to preserve the purity of the church; second, to restore the individual. It apparently worked in Corinth.

Paul's second letter to the Corinthians indicates the man repented. The church was to respond by overwhelming him with love: "The punishment inflicted on him by the majority is sufficient for him. Now instead, you ought to forgive and comfort him, so that he will not be overwhelmed by excessive sorrow. I urge you, therefore, to reaffirm your love for him" (2 Cor. 2:6–8).

Keep in mind, we hold Christians, not *non*-Christians, accountable to Christian values. The apostle Paul made that clear:

> I have written you in my letter not to associate with sexually immoral people—not at all meaning the people of this world who are immoral, or the greedy and swindlers, or idolaters. In that case you would have to leave this world. But now I am writing you that you must not associate with anyone who calls himself a brother but is sexually immoral or greedy, an idolater or a slanderer, a drunkard or a swindler. With such a man do not even eat. What business is it of mine to judge those outside the church? Are you not to judge those inside? God will judge those outside. "Expel the wicked man from among you" (1 Cor. 5:9–13).

Tim learned the value of mutual accountability a few years ago. Struggling with a temptation, he mentioned it to a fellow pastor whose eyes rose as he said, "You too? I thought I was alone."

Rather than tolerate the status quo, they entered into a relationship of mutual accountability, where each had the freedom to ask tough questions of the other, to be honest and still experience love and acceptance. Tough love drove out any chance of secular tolerance between these Christian brothers. The result? Great progress for both of them.

David has found in his marriage that tough love sometimes requires talking about difficult things. Kim, his wife, once noted that stress increased at mealtimes. She took the initiative and pointed it out to her husband. David acknowledged his responsibility for the problem and did something about it. Had Kim remained silent, tolerating unacceptable conditions, the stress might still prevail!

Part Three

Attitudes Toward Self

Chapter Nine

I Want It and I Want It Now

Instant Satisfaction Clashes with
Delayed Gratification

John and Sam: both young, both newly married, both with similar salaries. Although they started in much the same way, their stories finished very differently.

John rejoiced in earning a princely sum for his new bride. They covered their budget and had a surplus of $200 per week. John had little trouble spending the extra on restaurants, movies, tools, books, magazines, furniture, knick-knacks, gifts, travel, and sport. John lived right up to his means with his motto, *carpe diem*—"seize the day."

Sam made the same kind of money. But Sam decided to invest the extra cash for his retirement, for that time when he wouldn't be able to earn in the same way. So he and his wife lived more modestly, purchased more carefully, and waited longer to acquire things. They were comfortable, but careful.

As both neared retirement age, John owned more items

and had traveled to more places than Sam but faced lean years with little saved for the "rainy day" season of his life. Sam felt secure. Ten thousand dollars invested each year for a modest 5 percent return for forty-five years yielded a retirement nest egg of $1.63 million.

You may know these two men, but you may not have considered the fundamentally different values that motivated them. Instant satisfacation drove John. Sam had learned the value of delayed gratification.

CULTURE'S VALUE

What It Is

Our culture values instant gratification. We don't want to wait for anything. We expect a quick solution to every problem, a quick fix for every broken thing, a quick recovery from every sickness and a quick response to our every desire.

It's for Real

Our need for speed permeates life. We make a quick stop at Starbucks for coffee instead of brewing our own, eat fast food, and spend quick credit, all to minimize delays. Internet service providers lure us by promising higher speed and a shorter time for downloads. People no longer reserve sexual experience for marriage. Why wait?

The heavy debt that people carry today expresses our "buy now, pay later" mentality. The total U.S. consumer debt in 1951, *excluding* home mortgages, totaled just over $25 million.

In 2001, it passed $1,701 million. Bankruptcies have quadrupled over the past two decades. The need to have everything "now" is wreaking havoc in many lives.

Instant gratification is entrenched in our culture. We want and expect speed. Some of us grew up in homes where we jokingly said at mealtimes, "Around here it's the quick and the hungry." We say this in jest, but we live like that.

Emails have eliminated communication delays. David's letters from Tennessee to Western Australia in the 1980s took two weeks to arrive and another ten days for a reply to make its way back to the United States. Now, with instant messaging, voice mail, and email, we hardly have to wait for answers. And don't we grow very impatient if we don't hear *now*?

Retailers and advertisers exploit this impulsiveness with offers to "buy now and make no payments for twelve months." Or "we'll finance your car no matter how bad your credit record." We expect our pizza in 12–15 minutes, a weight loss program that will shed twenty pounds in ten days, tickets to the ballgame without waiting in line, and to be millionaires before we reach thirty. We want it, and we want it now.

The Payoffs

The fast life obviously benefits us. We can *pack more into our lives*. If we are not waiting here, we can be going there. The quicker we can move past this task, the quicker we arrive at the next item on life's agenda. In days gone by, we might have spent the evening hours cutting wood to build a fire or shelling beans for canning. Those same hours now require simply setting the thermostat, ordering out for pizza, loading the dishwasher, catching the eleven o'clock news, checking our email, and maybe building a model train set. We can surely pack in a lot.

Instant gratification comes from living at high speed. Not satisfaction of the soul but of our greed, appetites, or lusts. At least for the moment. If I'm hungry, get me the food fast to satisfy me. If I want a new car, let me drive it off the lot right now and I'll be happy. If I'm burning with passion, let me find instant intimacy to quell that appetite.

Instant gratification makes us *feel powerful.* Like the king of old who clicked his fingers and servants immediately appeared to meet his every need, we enjoy it when people rush to serve us—whether it's the waiter, the saleswoman, or the politician when it's time for reelection. Demanding and commanding quick attention massages our egos.

The Costs

But speed costs us. When our culture ceases to wait patiently *for* each other and we hastily wait *on* each other, *self-absorption takes over.* Our pace of life isolates us from each other and undermines communication and community. We don't build the richest elements in life and relationships in an instant. Self-absorption becomes our number-one enemy because relationships take time to develop.

Speed doesn't always benefit us. Drugs that give us instant pain relief may mask signals that our body tries to send. A fast-acting, pain-killing injection into the ankle of an athlete may simply let her damage the joint further if she continues to run.

Fast food may save us time, but it offers minimal nutrition for health. Automatic sprinklers in the garden may save us the additional time that hand-watering would require, but they can also rob us of the restorative calm and quiet of being among our plants.

Our culture rephrases the old adage that "good things come to those who wait" to "harm can come to those who wait." Instant gratification can ruin us. Tens of thousands of families across the Western world face dire financial straits because of their incapacity for waiting. They have sunk so deep into debt to have everything *now* that, ironically, they have become more likely to *lose* everything, including their marriages and friendships.

But even with all the dangers, we still expect instant satisfaction.

GOD'S VALUE

What It Is

Speed and instant gratification don't rank high as values in the kingdom of God. Indeed, the New Testament writers insist that the kingdom will be strongest when we willingly defer gratification. What a contrast!

It's for Real

Jesus taught his disciples to take the long view. On one occasion he said, "Blessed are you when people insult you and persecute you, and falsely say all kinds of evil against you because of Me. Rejoice and be glad, *for your reward in heaven is great*" (Matt. 5:11–12 NASB, emphasis added). Rather than compromise so people would immediately like them (instant gratification), his disciples were to accept the consequences of living for Christ and to look to a future time of fulfillment (deferred gratification).

Following the death and resurrection of Jesus, the apostle Paul wanted Jesus to return and usher in the new age of glory right away. So he prayed "Maranatha," *Come quickly* (1 Cor. 16:22 NASB). But while Paul longed for the quick return of Christ, he patiently toiled to accomplish the mission of Christ and urged his readers to live with perseverance and hope. Indeed, we usually cannot instantly achieve great things.

"Let us rejoice in hope of the glory of God. And not only this, but let us exult in our tribulations, knowing that tribulation brings about perseverance; and perseverance, proven character; and proven character, hope; and hope does not disappoint" (Rom. 5:2–5).

The apostle Peter also writes of self-control and perseverance (see 2 Peter 1:6). James writes in his letter about the perfecting effect of perseverance (see James 1:4). These verses speak specifically about persecution and trials, but they have a wider application. We will be unlikely to take the "long view" in one or two areas of life if we opt for the "short view" in the rest of our life.

Learning to wait helps us submit to God's timing. The psalmist learned that trying to make it all happen *now*, in his own strength, produced only frustration. He heard the Lord saying, "Cease striving—be still—and know that I am God" (Ps. 46:10 NASB). Instant gratification really stems from our desire to control life, but those in the kingdom of God live where he reigns. That means, in part, that we accept his timing. I may want a new car now, but I curb my impulsiveness and take time to consider the Lord and my priorities.

This clearly calls us to a different set of expectations and a different lifestyle. When we add this value of delayed gratification, what the Bible calls hope, to the principles of giving, sharing, simplicity, and contentment, we gain a deep and powerful foundation for living.

The Payoffs

Learning to wait yields multiple advantages. Peter, Paul, and James tell us that perseverance produces quality character. Persistence and patience perfect and complete us. The child who always gets his way grows to be precocious, not generous. The less we learn to wait, the more demanding we become. And that hinders rather than helps us.

Learning to pause and evaluate preserves us from foolish decisions. How many exercise bikes lie idle in home garages? You may have one! Many people spend big bucks on a stationary bike and use it fewer than twenty times. Why? We hear the salesman who promises fast weight-loss or quick fitness. So we buy without considering the need for a change of *lifestyle*. Now the bike sits idle.

God knows that deferred gratification produces deeper enjoyment. If we never have to wait, we never really appreciate. We won't value things the same way. We won't enjoy them to the same degree. Constant snacking will not satisfy like a hearty meal on an empty stomach. That becomes a metaphor for life.

The Costs

We experience costs with this countercultural living. Peer-group pressure makes it difficult to swim against the tide of impulsiveness. When everyone around us buys the latest, greatest, best, and biggest, we also want it—and want it now. Our children can especially place pressure on us since they soak up the surrounding culture like sponges.

Deferred gratification also requires considerable self-discipline, another fairly uncommon trait in our society. It challenges us if we are not used to it. Saying "No" to others can be hard enough, but saying "No" to ourselves can approach impossibility. Still, God has made this a core value in his kingdom.

LIVING IT OUT

We see the contrast between instant satisfaction and delayed gratification in two common phrases: "Tomorrow never comes" (instant satisfaction) and "Today is the first day of the rest of your life" (delayed gratification). The first phrase drives us to act desperately and hastily on every impulse. The second phrase allows us to build and wait, perhaps laying a foundation for what lies ahead. We tend to *over*estimate what we can do in the short-term and *under*estimate what we can do in the long-term.

Building a long-lasting and rewarding marriage requires delayed gratification. The need for instant satisfaction produces tension, financial woes, unfaithfulness, or escapism through drugs, alcohol, and entertainment. These things rob us of what God intended for us.

Furthermore, when we constantly succumb to our appetites, we will likely find ourselves overeating, underexercising, and in generally poor physical condition. The apostle Paul said, "I discipline my body and make it my slave, so that, after I have preached to others, I myself will not be disqualified" (1 Cor. 9:27 NASB).

We might want to teach this principle in simple ways. For example, as a family, we can teach our children to wait until everyone is served before we start eating. Not just as a courtesy, but to teach our children that higher values exist than their own appetites. At Christmas, rather than have everyone rip open their gifts simultaneously, take turns to open gifts and watch others enjoy their discoveries. These small steps will ingrain in us a new set of values.

Tim's family tends to marry late, but as he entered his mid-twenties, he discovered he became pickier, with fewer females to pick from. Several potential candidates didn't work out, and he thought he might break the family record for delaying marital bliss. He didn't particularly look forward to being a perpetual bachelor, nor did he want to marry just to be married. Several "candidates" could have met that goal. In numerous conversations, God seemed gently to say, "Go slow. Follow me. Don't get stressed about it." Then, at thirty, he became the associate pastor at a California church, fell in love with one of the sponsors of the college group, and married his life's mate at thirty-one. He discovered that the best gratification comes at the right time; that some things are worth waiting for.

How about you? Will you commit to countering our culture's emphasis on getting it right now?

But It Feels So Good

*Pleasing Self (Hedonism) Clashes
with Sacrifice*

Every year, hundreds of pleasure-seekers flock to Club Hedonism in Jamaica to indulge their desires. The publicity states, "This resort was created as a reward for all those times you've had to deny your basic instincts. In these lush gardens of pure pleasure, the word 'no' is seldom heard."

Club Hedonism encourages the hedonistic impulses of our culture. And while we followers of Christ may avoid visiting such a place, the pursuit of pleasure remains high on our agenda because it ranks high on our culture's agenda.

In 2002, pop-star Kylie Minogue penned a song entitled "It Feels So Good," which became the album title and a popular track for British girl-band Atomic Kitten. That song title reflects the desperate craving of our culture for everything to feel so good.

Judith Aronson presented a workshop at the twentieth annual conference on the psychology of the self that asked,

"How can something that feels so good be a bad thing?" What felt so good? Pedophilic behavior. She challenged the prevailing view that all pleasure must be morally acceptable. Such is the distorting influence of hedonism today.

CULTURE'S VALUE

What It Is

You've heard it said many times and may have said it yourself. "We were just having fun." Police hear it when they pull over drag racers roaring through suburban streets. Parents hear it when they ask their teenagers about drinking or drugs. Courts hear it when they prosecute date-rapists, arsonists, thrill-killers, and others. We use those words in many contexts to justify our actions. We measure our quality of life by enjoyment, fun, and pleasure.

Contemporary Western culture places a premium on pleasure. We want pleasurable sensations and seek them in food, sports, entertainment, and sex. We now regard "creature comforts" as inalienable rights. We *deserve* pleasure and comfort and are fully entitled to it.

On the reverse side of the coin, we do everything possible to minimize pain. Consequently, we've become the most medicated society in human history as we seek to avoid every ache and to cure every ailment.

It's for Real

The money Americans spend on exotic food and film, sports and recreational drugs, vacations and electronic games, and toys and household comforts staggers us. Such nonessentials annually account for hundreds of billions of dollars in the U.S. economy The 2001 film *Castaway*, for example, brought in over $233 million at the box office as well as an additional $121 million in video/DVD rentals and sales. Think about this: One film grossed more than a third of a billion dollars! In 2000, the average American household spent 9.8 percent of its income on entertainment. Pleasure is big business.

Pleasure has become an overpowering value in our culture. That reality perhaps explains why, in 2002, "the happiest place on earth," Disneyland, filled its park in Southern California with 12.7 million guests. The theme park averaged nearly 35,000 visitors per day, despite a $45 admission price in the midst of an economic recession.

The Payoffs

Pleasure produces an emotional high. It feels good. The pain and stress of this world overwhelm us; pleasure provides a counterbalance on several levels.

First, *we feel psychologically better*. Pleasure imparts a positive outlook on life. It defers or dispels pain because the two cannot coexist. Enjoyment, happiness, and satisfaction create a pleasant, even if temporary, environment. We *enjoy* having fun.

Second, pleasure *yields physical benefits*. Researchers tell us that laughing activates the hypothalamus, pituitary, and adrenal glands. That action releases endorphins—natural chemicals—into the bloodstream that make us feel better. The body relaxes and disease-fighting cells dramatically increase.

Laughter and pleasure may be a good adjunct therapy for sickness. But the effect of pleasure surpasses the mere therapeutic value. Pleasure also attracts us by its sheer physical delight. Ice cream *tastes* good on the tongue. A hot tub *feels* good on an aching body. A massage *relaxes* tight muscles.

But what is the ultimate benefit of hedonism? *It helps us escape.* Even temporary pleasure distracts us from the pain of life. Pleasure enables us to forget hardship and stress. It may not *resolve* our problems, but it does *defer* them, and that feels good. The benefits, however, come with costs.

The Costs

When we combine hedonism with the cultural values of competition, individualism, and selfishness, it can lead to a lifestyle of *reckless abandon.* The rapid spread of HIV/AIDS is largely from the result of unrestrained hedonism. Pleasure without responsibility kills millions of people in our world today. Infected people often transmit the virus due to their compulsion to satisfy their own desires. Hedonistic recklessness, on a somewhat less dramatic level, has contributed to the increase of obesity within Western society. Many of us love to eat with little regard for the health implications. Overeating has become characteristic of our age and has resulted in dramatic increases in heart disease and other health complications. In fact, in January 2003 the *Journal of the American Medical Association* reported that being obese at age twenty can lop a whopping twenty years off our lives. Lifestyles of reckless abandon prove, literally, to be short-lived.

Hedonism also breeds *insensitivity to the hurts of others.* It's tough, after all, to eat at the buffet table while discussing the malnourished and starving children of the world. Consequently, we talk football or retirement planning so we can enjoy our luxury. We ignore the hurts of others so we can persist in our pleasures. What adulterer keeps a photo of his wife handy during an affair? He won't allow her pain to diminish his passion or pleasure.

Another cost of hedonism causes us, at our peril, to *deny our own pain*. It serves as a mask, not as a remedy, and thwarts emotional and physical healing. When we go to the doctor for help, we obviously don't take painkillers before we leave home. How will the doctor pinpoint the problem when we get to his office? The use of drugs or alcohol similarly serves merely to bury emotional pain and simply delays the needed healing process.

Hedonism also provides *a false standard* to evaluate ministry. Tim made some leadership changes on the worship team at his church that led to a difficult transition. One of the members resigned from the team saying, "It's just not fun anymore." It was important to address the friction that resulted from the transition. The team also needed to learn that "having fun" is not the purpose for doing ministry.

Hedonism ultimately produces *cultural decay*. The ancient Greco-Roman philosophers advocated self-mastery. They saw the dangers of hedonism and taught that pleasure-seeking produced a softness and weakness that resulted in moral laxity, personal destruction, and cultural decay. There is another way to live: a better way.

GOD'S VALUE

What It Is

The kingdom value of self-sacrifice contrasts with the hedonism of our Western culture. Of course, God doesn't oppose pleasure. He created us to enjoy it. Pleasure in itself is not bad. After all, God himself looked at creation at the end of each day and declared it "good." He took pleasure in its beauty.

Our preoccupation with pleasure as the primary goal of life, however, has little merit. While our faith invites God's blessing, we must begin with sacrificial obedience to the Lord.

It's for Real

Jesus wanted his followers to experience life to the full (see John 10:10). He once said, "I have told you this so that my joy may be in you and that your joy may be complete" (John 15:11). The experience of a full life is quite different from a search for pleasure. Pleasure-seeking, as an end in itself, leads us to a dead end.

True fulfillment, in one of the great kingdom ironies, comes from giving, not getting. Jesus said, "It is more blessed to give than to receive" (Acts 20:35). Such a sacrificial spirit flies in the face of hedonistic philosophy. We won't find fulfillment by seeking to satisfy our own desires but by practicing generosity and focusing outward toward the good of others. Jesus said on another occasion, "Whoever wants to save his life will lose it, but whoever loses his life for me will find it" (Matt. 16:25).

The great surprise we discover is that pleasure, satisfaction, peace, contentment, and joy are all byproducts of sacrifice and service. The apostle Paul wrote that "the kingdom of God is not a matter of eating and drinking, but of righteousness, peace and joy in the Holy Spirit" (Rom. 14:17). Our richest experiences come from submitting ourselves to the will of God and sacrificing control to the Spirit of God. Paul noted earlier in his life that when we walk by the Spirit, our lives produce the fruit of the Spirit, which includes joy (see Gal. 5:22). Real pleasure is a spin off of sacrifice.

But the Bible also teaches that, because of their destructive potential, we should avoid some pleasures. Eve yearned to eat the forbidden fruit in the Garden of Eden because the tree was good for food, a delight to the eyes, and desirable (see Gen. 3:6). It promised pleasure. She and Adam ate it without regard to the consequences. They ought to have sacrificed the pleasure of the fruit to retain the promise of God. We sometimes need to sacrifice pleasure for the sake of the blessing we want to retain. The apostle John recognized this truth nearly 2000 years ago:

> Everything in the world—the cravings of sinful
> man, the lust of his eyes and the boasting of what
> he has and does—comes not from the Father but
> from the world. The world and its desires pass
> away, but the man who does the will of God lives
> forever. (1 John 2:16–17)

On the one hand, true pleasure comes our way as we sacrifice our selfishness and choose to walk in step with the Spirit of God. On the other hand, we experience true blessing when we sacrifice the momentary pleasure that might destroy us.

The Payoffs

We should not overlook the paradox that, as we give away our lives, we find them. When we sacrifice, we unexpectedly experience life to the full. And all the promises the world has failed to keep find their fulfillment in us.

Self-sacrifice for God's sake enriches our psychological well-being. As we present our bodies as living and holy sacrifices to God (see Rom. 12:1), we find that we experience the peace that passes all understanding (see Phil. 4:7), and joy and contentment permeate us. We can manage well in all circumstances of life because Christ strengthens us inwardly (see Phil. 4:13). Worldly hedonism promises well-being but fails to deliver. A life of sacrifice to God delivers it all.

While hedonism provides an escape, it offers no lasting solutions. Physical comforts do not resolve relational difficulties or emotional stresses. As we sacrifice ourselves to follow the Spirit's leading, however, we discover that he is our supreme comforter and counselor (see John 14:16), empowerer (see Acts 1:8), and transformer (see Rom. 12:2). We can reject escapism when we experience permanent transformation on the inside that allows us to cope and excel in all of life.

The Costs

We discover life when we deny ourselves and die daily to our own desires and selfishness. Such a difficult task requires an intentionality that costs us something on a social level. Swimming against our culture's hedonistic current may strain our relationships and create awkward moments. For example, when our Bible school class plans a restaurant dinner as a social event, we may feel uncomfortable to suggest that we eat instead in a home and donate food to the hungry. Not every Bible school class wants to be aware of the hurts of the world. Similarly, the challenge to carpool to work or a sporting event for the sake of supporting the needy will encounter varying levels of puzzlement.

Our personal comfort has become sacrosanct. No one dares question it. Pleasure has become the new god of the age. The costs of smashing that idol can be significant. The costs of not confronting it, however, are even greater.

LIVING IT OUT

Living out the kingdom value of sacrifice will look different for each of us. Pursuit of this value will involve not just one or two large decisions but a multitude of small ones.

We periodically receive emails that tempt us with pornographic pleasure. A click of the mouse will open up some enticing sites. But these pleasures destroy our marriages and families, our ministries, and our ability to relate to people nonsexually. They, in the end, destroy our souls. Lots of pleasure, but more destruction.

The greatest defense is a rapid offense—the choice to sacrifice that destructive pleasure for a higher good. Let's make that sacrifice by immediately deleting and then blocking or filtering the email. We must sacrifice a temporary pleasure in order to pursue life and health. Welcome to the kingdom of God.

God intends for us to enjoy life to the full. We clearly ought not, therefore, pursue inappropriate pleasures. But we must also consider the excessive pursuit of *permissible* pleasures. Food, for instance, is a good thing, created by God and necessary for the body. But excessive eating, while delightful to the palate, doesn't help either our waistline or our heart. Further, it disregards the millions who have insufficient food for their daily needs. We might consider eating a little less so we can enjoy better health and give more away. The same could be said of smoking, drinking, movie-going, and other pleasures. Excess transforms pleasure into a foe.

Many desires arise within us every day. A multitude of pleasurable and comfortable experiences lie at our fingertips. We have no intention to throw cold water on every joy. We encourage you, however, to embrace purity and a spirit of sacrifice so that you might experience joy to the full. Kingdom values produce real life.

Chapter Eleven

You *Will* Do What I Say

Power Clashes with Submission

George earned his reputation as a hard-driving, "my way or the highway" boss. He frequently exchanged ideas with employees—"You come in with your ideas, and you'll leave with mine."

Sam worked under George as a computer programmer and rightly feared sharing his complaints with him. So he just worked slowly. Not slowly enough to be noticed, just enough to delay the completion of key projects. He developed great skill at identifying nonexistent glitches in the machines. George had no way of knowing.

In a different scenario, Charlene appeared to be the dutiful Christian wife, yet subtly manipulated her husband. She would grant or withhold physical affection, fix or not fix his favorite meals just to enforce her desire to be the "neck that turned the head of the house."

Brad blustered, shouted, and used the threat of physical power to keep his family in line. Although he had never struck nor directly threatened Charlene, she quivered inside when he became angry.

These four individuals shared far more in common than they could imagine.

CULTURE'S VALUE

What It Is

Despite their abundant differences, Bob, Sam, Charlene, and Brad each possessed a ferocious self-will, combined with a willingness to use their power to get their way. Our culture encourages our innate desire to get our own way and to control. As a result, we become drawn ever more deeply into the pit of power used for self.

It's for Real

We've heard phrases such as "survival of the fittest"; "if I don't look out for #1, no one will"; "take control of your life"; "knowledge is power."

Each of these plays to our instinctive craving to get our way. We each have needs that we want to meet. Each one of us has a will, desires, and preferences. Our self-will opposes other people even as it imposes upon them.

To get our way, we often use whatever power is available. Men typically use their position, voice, and physical strength. Women may use their attractiveness, charm, or words. We seek promotions at work to increase our power. Throughout our culture, we see people using power to get their way and to acquire more power.

The Payoffs

Power *helps us get our way*. We use power to manipulate others, and it works!

Power *allows us to ignore the needs of others*. We feel important and free to discount other people. Their value lies in how they meet our needs, not vice versa. The time, energy, and effort to look after others' needs, therefore, decrease.

Power also *advances our reputation and status*. The more powerful we become, the more influential we become. The control of other people addicts us.

The Costs

The pursuit of power ultimately leads us into a *battle of dueling wills*. Marriages become a struggle of who gets their way, as do the work environment and friendships. Relationships decay because we each push each other to meet our needs without regard for meeting theirs. When we control others, we usurp their will. It always produces conflict.

Our quest for power may also produce the surprising disadvantage of *getting our way*. What we think is best for us may not always be! When we act in the best interests of others, they often, in turn, benefit us. When we battle people, however, they usually give us little beyond what we force them to give. A need met by means of force means little in comparison to a need met by means of love.

GOD'S VALUE

What It Is

God designed us not to pursue power but to value submission. Our culture recoils at that concept. Even *Webster's Dictionary* defines it as, "acknowledgement of inferiority or dependence; humble or suppliant behavior; meekness; resignation. Acknowledgement of a fault; confession of error."

Not very attractive! That definition reflects our *cultural* value, not the *godly* one. Submission, as the Bible portrays it, means we voluntarily lift up the needs of others. We place the needs of others at the top of the heap. We sacrifice our needs in order to help others. In every arena, submission forms the foundation for effective relationships.

When God created humankind, he gave us dominion over everything else he created (see Gen. 1:28). But a world of difference exists between dominion and domination. *Dominion* means that we look out for the best interests of everything and everyone. *Domination* means we look out for our own interests. Not surprisingly, when Adam and Eve decided to grab for power—to become like God—they ended up in serious interpersonal conflict. They immediately tried to blame one another rather than submit either to God or each other. Thankfully, in God's kingdom, we seek to restore the original design.

It's for Real

Jesus provides the prime example of submission. Consider Philippians 2:5–8:

Your attitude should be the same as that of Christ
Jesus: Who, being in very nature God, did not
consider equality with God something to be
grasped, but made himself nothing, taking the
very nature of a servant, being made in human
likeness. And being found in appearance as a man,
he humbled himself and became obedient to
death—even death on a cross!

Look what Jesus yielded: equality with God the Father. He
submitted, at great personal cost, to our need for a Savior. Quite
a contrast to the use of power and control we see in our culture.
Being in very nature God, Jesus could have refused the job. He
could have called on thousands of angels to rescue him from the
cross. He could have attacked his aggressors. Instead of exercising
power and control, however, he submitted to our needs.

That provides the pattern for us, doesn't it? We need that
same attitude of submission to replace our self-will and our
self-absorbed pursuit of power. Let's explore selected verses
from Ephesians 5:21–6:9 that link submission to a wide range
of relationships:

Submit to one another out of reverence for Christ.
Wives, submit to your husbands as to the Lord. For
the husband is the head of the wife as Christ is the
head of the church…. *Husbands, love your wives,*
just as Christ loved the church and gave himself
up for her…. *Children, obey your parents* in the
Lord, for this is right. "Honor your father and
mother … ." *Fathers, do not exasperate your children*;

instead, bring them up in the training and
instruction of the Lord. *Slaves, obey your earthly
masters* with respect and fear, and with sincerity of
heart, just as you would obey Christ.... And
masters, treat your slaves in the same way. Do not
threaten them.... (emphasis added).

The opening sentence in this passage communicates God's
value of relationships: all should submit to others. We ought
not insist on our own way. We must not use power to achieve
our ends. The text next provides details on how each of us
submits. Wives yield to the husbands. Husbands yield to the
wives. Children learn how to submit to the parents, and the
parents also give consideration to the children. Even slaves
and masters should treat each other with mutual respect.

What did we *not* see in that passage? Power. Control.
Domination. We found, rather, a mutual commitment to meet
the needs of others. Our intent is not to enable their addictions
but to meet their valid needs. Submission means we place their
needs on a level above our own. It's not "us against them," but
"us *with* them." Most importantly, it is "us *for* them."

The Payoffs

When we submit to one another, how do we benefit?

First, we have an *antidote to the aggression* that the need for
power and control breeds. We attack power at its root by
giving it up. We relinquish personal benefit and power as we
give priority to the needs of others.

Second, we see healthy *relationships prosper.* Rather than
dueling self-wills, we enjoy the benefits of mutual submission,

where we each try to outdo the other in bringing good (see Rom. 12:10). Whether marriage, or family, or work, we move beyond ourselves.

Honestly, though, we do face some disadvantages.

The Costs

Most obviously, submission *goes against our grain*. Most of us don't naturally yield to others. By our very nature, we tend to look out for ourselves and to suspect others. Our culture trains us to do this. Retraining our ingrained tendencies takes time.

We have to *lay down our own dreams*. Tim would love to live in the mountains of Colorado, but the altitude, the cold, and distance from the grandkids makes Sheila much less eager. As Tim submits to her needs, he lets go of the mountains for a greater good. He does, however, lose something he would personally enjoy.

We may also *feel like a doormat*. Recall our culture's definitions of submission: surrender; obedience to people; suppliant behavior; resignation; yielding; inferiority. Those terms don't thrill us! As long as we accept those definitions, every time we submit to another person we feel exploited. That feeling will persist until we realize that only the strong can voluntarily submit. The weak merely give in.

LIVING IT OUT

As our first step in practicing submission, we conduct a *ruthless self-evaluation*. How deeply have I allowed the pursuit of power and control to imbed itself in my life? I (Tim) once felt particularly bold and asked a good friend to help in this process. A friend pointed out to me one way I seemed to manipulate people. I honestly hadn't been aware of it, but my friend helped me to see the truth. I have since then begun to consciously combat this fault.

Second, we *make the changes*. We put the needs of others above our own. We act on them. The apostle Paul wrote, "Do nothing out of selfish ambition or vain conceit, but in humility consider others better than yourselves. Each of you should look not to your own interests, but to the interests of others" (Phil. 2:3–4).

Start living a life of submission; watch how God transforms your attitudes toward others. Some Christian men may need to consider that their career path is not automatically the dominant one in the marriage. Open discussion and mutual decision-making, not simply presumption or rigid expectation, should determine the various roles within a marriage. Such considerations move us toward mutual submission and away from power playing. But it requires conversation and communication.

I (David) have learned over the years that team leadership requires affirmation more than power. When I try to control groups of people, I encounter automatic resistance. But when I listen, respect, and submit to the creativity of the group, a remarkable shift in productivity and effectiveness happens.

Examine your relationships: family, workplace, church, and other social settings. What values do you mostly display? Power or submission? We find the kingdom of God in the latter.

Chapter Twelve

Whatever Works

Pragmatism Clashes with Obedience

Christina Silvas wants the best for her daughter. So she enrolled her daughter in Capitol Christian School of Sacramento, California, an institution of learning dedicated to an effective partnership with parents to provide a values-based education. To achieve that, parents sign a covenant that they will pursue a lifestyle consistent with the school's values. Silvas agreed to sign.

But for a single mother, the $400 monthly tuition places a strain on an already tight budget. So, three nights a week, when her daughter stays with her father, Christina takes it off. Working as a stripper helps pay the tuition at the Christian school.

How ironic! Silvas had a great goal: a values-based Christian education for her daughter. She developed a practical plan to meet that goal: taking her clothes off three nights a week. She reasoned that the end justifies the means. And while Silvas agreed wholeheartedly with the position of the school—parents and the school need to work together—she couldn't quite understand why her behavior upset the school administration.

CULTURE'S VALUE

What It Is

Christina Silvas exemplifies the pragmatism that saturates our culture. Some people use the word utilitarianism—anything useful is fine. Rather than allow certain values to determine right from wrong, pragmatism asserts that only the results matter. General values are less important than what works. Pragmatism tells us to do whatever it takes. Do what works. If the end product is good, then the process is acceptable.

According to pragmatism, an act that most Christians would consider immoral can be moral if the outcome justifies it. Methods possess no morality in and of themselves.

It's for Real

Pragmatism is alive and well at the core of Western society. We hear it reflected in common statements: "As long as it all works out in the end"; "The end justifies the means"; "It's easier to ask for forgiveness than ask for permission"; "Just do whatever it takes." Pragmatism and a Christian worldview clash, however, when a good purpose (a Christian education) conflicts with the means of achieving it (working as a stripper).

This conflict permeates our culture. David knows a single parent who routinely shoplifted to provide her child with toys and clothes so the daughter would not feel deprived. A worthy goal, but an unworthy process. In the workplace, we may exaggerate our résumé to get a job. Landing the job justifies the lies. Employment is a worthy goal; the pragmatism that compromises our integrity—get a job, whatever it takes—is not.

A Christian organization uses unauthorized mailing lists to promote its services and to seek donors. Justification seems easy. After all, society needs its valuable services. Besides, no individual makes a profit from it. This kind of reasoning downplays the theft of someone else's property.

The piracy of music and computer software is a contemporary example of pragmatism. When we use music or software for personal use or a "noble cause"—a classroom presentation or a church service—we quickly rationalize our way around the biblical command to obey the laws of the land that prohibit stealing. Pragmatism triumphs over obedience.

In May 2002, the actor Michael J. Fox testified at a congressional hearing on Parkinson's disease. Visibly trembling from effects of the condition, he argued to expand embryonic stem cell research because of its potential to help Parkinson's sufferers. He made no references to the destruction of human embryonic life. That issue deserves debate, but Fox ignored it. Why? The practical benefits had more importance. Only the end result matters.

The Payoffs

Many benefits exist with pragmatism. *In business*, emphasizing the bottom line often enhances the bottom line, at least for the short-term. Enron executives looked after their personal bottom lines, raking in huge bonuses before the company went bankrupt. Pragmatism benefited their personal bottom line even though it undermined the investments of their stockholders.

In relationships, this attitude of "whatever works" can be quite productive for a time. We may enter and maintain relationships based on the benefits those relationships temporarily produce for us. A man seeking peace with his wife may say "yes, yes, yes" to every accusation and statement she makes simply to get the storm to blow over, with little regard for true communication or reconciliation. He achieves temporary peace but sows the seeds of long-term dysfunction. A woman who desires security may allow physical abuse, ignoring its effects on her and her children. She feels trapped by the need for food and shelter and compromises important values to meet those needs.

We are more likely in every arena in life to get specific results when we focus on results *alone*. And when we achieve a specific result—regardless of the pathway to it—we're successful. That's pragmatic.

The Costs

At its worst, pragmatism *ignores the impact on others*, focusing on the benefit to us. It is fundamentally self-centered. We place either our individual or our group's benefit above others. Consequently, it fragments society and distances us from each other. Life is a journey, not a destination, which pragmatism fails to understand.

Pragmatism also tends to be *short-sighted*. We evaluate the outcome for the *now*, with little thought for the future. The Enron executives' preoccupation with their personal benefits *today* ignored inevitable long-term damage to the company and the national economy. They also failed to consider other long-term unpleasant results, such as prison and heavy fines.

Pragmatism is simply *another form of relativism*. The need to follow God's moral commands will disappear if we can rationalize practical benefits. Rather than asking, "What's the right thing?" we ask, "What will work?" We then do whatever promises to benefit us the most. The noble definition of utilitarianism as "whatever brings the greatest benefit to the greatest number of people" is fundamentally flawed. Killing a thousand people to save five thousand people is not necessarily the right thing to do. Likewise, lying to someone to "protect him from the truth" is of questionable merit.

Both pragmatism and relativism require us to abandon absolute ethics in order to achieve and justify our desires. Such abandonment can lead to anarchy, where each individual establishes a lifestyle based on personal benefit.

GOD'S VALUE

What It Is

In sharp contrast to the value our culture places on pragmatism, God honors obedience. And our obedience is not based on what works but on what God says. We adopt his perspective of life. God wants us to apply a solid core of ethical values in every situation. Doing so will help us to avoid the tempting bias of pragmatism. Unethical means never in the long run produce a good outcome. Why not? Because unethical means injure others while blessing a few. This process ultimately produces mistrust and suspicion in the community.

Pragmatism, at its most basic level, assumes that we know better than God what works best. Obedience leads us to follow God's advice, even when it doesn't make sense to us, even when it may not seem to work in the short-term. Obedience exalts God; pragmatism exalts individuals. One is faith-based; the other is sight-based.

"What works" is of secondary importance to Christians. Many things work for a short time and in limited ways. But the long-term negatives often outweigh the short-term positives. Recall the story about the customized motorcycle in our opening chapter. Short-term benefits included winning the motorcycle show. Long-term costs included breaking down on a road trip. Pragmatism—whatever it takes to win the show—compromised the expert's design and resulted in breakdown.

It's for Real

The Old Testament yields many great examples of the pitfalls of pragmatism and the blessings of obedience. In 2 Kings 5, a foreign soldier named Naaman provides a marvelous example.

Naaman was afflicted with leprosy and heard that a prophet of Israel, Elisha, could cure him. Elisha's recommended course of treatment? Naaman was to dip himself seven times into the Jordan River. Naaman was incensed at this insult to his intelligence; it just didn't make sense. This could not work!

He finally tried the treatment. The cure happened. What was the key? To obey, even when it doesn't seem to make sense, and other options seem more logical. The principle that "God knows best" underlies this story and provides the foundation for obedience—God best determines what is right and wrong. That hits at the center of our faith, as we often have to trust God's wisdom in the face of the cultural wisdom we hear every day.

Indeed, God has always expected his people in his kingdom to obey him. When God tells us to obey, he doesn't make the command conditional: "Do this, unless you can find a better, quicker, or easier way."

God's original covenant with the people of Israel required their obedience: I'll do good for you, and you obey me. "Then the LORD said: 'I am making a covenant with you. Before all your people I will do wonders never before done in any nation in all the world. The people you live among will see how awesome is the work that I, the LORD, will do for you. Obey what I command you today'" (Exod. 34:10–11).

The Lord said, in essence, "Don't make excuses; don't get pragmatic. Don't try to determine right and wrong for yourselves. Just obey what I say, and I'll bless you."

That principle also undergirds the New Covenant, which centers on a relationship with Jesus as both Savior and Lord. "If you love me, you will obey what I command" (John 14:15). Jesus links obedience with love throughout John chapters 14 and 15.

Remember the opposite of obedience? Pragmatism. A

man named Saul became a follower of Jesus. He had previously stood out among his contemporaries in Judaism and had a bright future as a leader in Israel. But God called him to take the good news of Jesus to the Gentile world. Paul, as we better know him, could have ignored the call. He was already on track to comfort, popularity, and political power. The call to obedience would prove costly—the loss of everything he had worked so hard to get and to become. But for the past 2,000 years, Paul's obedience has impacted the entire world. It's not about what we *think* will work. It's about what God *tells* us to do.

The Payoffs

When we place obedience to God above pragmatism, we benefit. First, we *access the expert's design for life*. Our premise: God knows best how life works. He created it. Obedience, because we can't see the big picture, sometimes doesn't seem to have practical benefits. Obedience occasionally quickly benefits us personally. Sometimes it takes longer. God's way, however, *is always* the best way. In fact, in the long-term, obedience produces *better* results than pragmatism.

Obedience also leads to full joy. We might expect this, if obedience links us to God's design for life. Jesus said to his followers in John 15:11 (NASB), "These things I have spoken to you [these commands I have given you and asked you to obey] that My joy may be in you, and that your joy may be made full." It's a wonderful promise. Obedience doesn't produce drudgery, but joy. What an unexpected twist. Obedience transcends momentary satisfaction in every way.

We see, last of all, that obedience leads to *enhanced relationships*. Why? We avoid the inherent self-centeredness of pragmatism. We become thoughtful of others. We move beyond focusing on the practical consequences that benefit us and rely upon what God says will bring good to all those we contact.

The Costs

Obedience, at the same time, may yield short-term disadvantages. After examining countless homes, Carl found just the right house, made an acceptable offer, and applied for a real estate loan. The loan application required a listing of all debts, and Carl debated about mentioning a $40,000 loan from a family member. Being in the family, no one outside knew of it. But since he was committed to obeying the kingdom value of honesty, Carl put it down.

That loan and its monthly payments disqualified him for the real estate loan. Short-term, he lost the house and the home seller got upset. But Carl didn't compromise his integrity. A house passed up; a character intact. When we commit to obedience, we sometimes lose something: a loan, a relationship, a job promotion. Obedience has its price.

LIVING IT OUT

What might be the consequences of valuing obedience over pragmatism?

A church won't primarily evaluate prospective programs on the basis of projected attendance increases. It will ask, instead, if the methods and underlying principles reflect biblical values. We will evaluate candidates for church leadership, not by how much they give, but by their level of obedience to the Lord in many areas of their life. Political considerations give way to obedience considerations.

Christian organizations might reconsider some of their marketing and promotional strategies, even at the risk of losing significant contributions.

Christian politicians might look to deeper values in analyzing issues rather than to the polls. Such deeper values will touch such issues as embryonic stem cell research, abortion, and business ethics. Votes should never be the primary consideration.

We as individuals would seek to obey God's Word and way in everything. We would place more emphasis on those findings than pragmatism.

Our culture covets a good bottom line. Sometimes, however, the methods used to achieve the bottom line violate biblical mandates. We must be willing to seek God's values and to obey them at all stages, regardless of the practical implications.

Chapter Thirteen

The Sky Is My Limit

Ambition Clashes with Honoring God

Brent was an everyday twenty-something. Married. Two children. Ambitious.

He vowed to become a millionaire before his mid-thirties. He wanted to provide well for his family and prove himself to the world. He was devoted to his dreams and determined to achieve financial security. His wife, as a result, lived most of the week without a husband, and his children lived without a father.

The glass ceiling at work frustrated Mandy. She would prove herself in this man's world, whatever it took. She thought nothing of manipulating men and trampling on women to get where she wanted to go. No one would stop her. She wanted the top position in the company. Her ambition left a trail littered with broken relationships, angry people, and jealous coworkers as she moved up the corporate ladder.

You know these two. They model a value that our culture widely embraces—ambition. The sky is our limit.

It's for Real

The *Random House Dictionary* defines ambition as "an earnest desire for some type of achievement or distinction, as power, fame, wealth, etc." That desire has become a permanent feature of our day.

Ambition can take many forms, but it usually boils down to the pursuit of power, wealth, fame, or some combination of all three. We respect the ambition to own a business, to be elected, to be recognized, to be affluent, or to be the CEO. We tend to soften the concept of raw ambition for our children by helping them to "chase a dream," "pursue a goal," "make something of their lives," or to "reach their full potential." You recognize the clichés. Each of them puts a positive spin on ambition.

Our educational systems further reinforce this value. We've heard from our earliest school days that life is about survival of the fittest. We naturally strive to be the fittest, reach the top, go to college, be the best, and to succeed.

The Payoffs

Ambition offers great rewards. Ambitious people often *produce*. They get things done. They are the movers and shakers. They are achievers. They also benefit society, producing new products, developing new systems, and stimulating growth. These visionaries and entrepreneurs pursue their dreams. Ambitious people, therefore, stand out from the crowd. They get attention and fame. They receive the privileges and perks.

We parents generally want our children to stand out rather than to blend into insignificance. We want the best for them. We urge them to strive for the top. If we can infect our children with the ambition virus, we reason that we have given them the motivation to make something of their lives.

The Costs

This cultural value comes with high costs, especially *broken relationships*. We find too many Brents and Mandys in our culture. Ambitious people often hike a trail of pain and dysfunctional relationships.

Anna Mann, who in 1998 divorced global media magnate Rupert Murdoch after thirty-one years of marriage, blamed the disintegration of their marriage on ambition. Murdoch refused to slow down, to settle in one place, or to release his children from the huge expectations he had placed on them, even though he had accumulated $12 billion in assets. Blind ambition is an insatiable taskmaster.

Isolation accompanies ambition. The close connection between ambition and competition means that ambitious people often sacrifice relationships to achieve their personal goals and desires.

Raw ambition may also lead to the *compromise of our values*. Consider the extreme example of Colombian drug cartels. The drug lords are driven by an unrestrained, deep-seated thirst for power and wealth. Life—everyone else's—loses all value. Elsewhere, the pornography barons of the world pursue power and wealth with no consideration for how their industry affects individuals, families, and marriages around the world. They demean and degrade people to achieve their goals. We face a similar temptation to compromise when a promotion or a bonus is tied to performance figures we know are not accurate. Ambition can cloud our integrity.

No parent in the world would urge their son or daughter to settle for mediocrity. But mediocrity is not the sole alternative to ambition.

GOD'S VALUE

What It Is

The Bible does not provide a high view of ambition. The apostle John spoke of the evils that beset our world and described them as rooted in "the lust of the flesh and the lust of the eyes and the boastful pride of life" (1 John 2:16 NASB). Wanting, coveting, envy, greed, or pride often drive ambition.

God's values motivate us to replace personal ambition with a decision to honor God above all else. No other ambition should supplant this one. Does the relinquishing of selfish ambition require us to drop out of Western society and join a monastery in Egypt? Not so!

It's for Real

The apostle Paul wrote to the believers at Philippi, "Do nothing from selfishness or conceit, but with humility of mind regard one another as more important than yourself" (Phil. 2:3 NASB). He rightly understood that the ambitions of this world can divide and destroy.

The countercultural alternative to worldly ambition is, in the words of Jesus, to seek first God's kingdom and righteousness (see Matt. 6:33). Paul later exhorted the Ephesians to learn what pleases God rather themselves (see Eph. 5:10). Paul likewise instructed the Colossian believers to set their minds on things above, not on the things of earth (see Col. 3:2). Here's why.

As we seek to honor God and make his glory our exclusive ambition, we learn to depend on him and trust him as never before. We recognize that an abundant life results from a partnership with the Lord, not from our own solo performance.

The renowned prophet Samuel reminded his Israelite audience long before Christ came that the Lord had said, "Those who honor me I will honor" (1 Sam. 2:30). That principle relates to today as much as in the year 1050 B.C., when Samuel uttered it.

The prophet Jeremiah looked upon the Promised Land nearly five hundred years later as the Babylonian Empire overran it. He gave this word from God to the Jews, "'I know the plans that I have for you … plans for welfare and not for calamity to give you a future and a hope" (Jer. 29:11 NASB). Rather than ambitiously craft their own future, God wanted them to trust in his provision and seek to honor him.

Trusting God does not lead to passivity. Neither does it justify mediocrity. On the contrary, Paul set the highest of standards when he wrote, "Whatever you do, do your work heartily, as for the Lord, rather than for men" (Col. 3:23 NASB). Our desire to honor God will cause us to pursue excellence, but with a vastly different motivation than the desire to honor ourselves.

The kingdom principle of seeking and serving the Lord above all other ambitions runs consistently throughout the Bible.

The Payoffs

This kingdom principle will change our lives. Personal ambition forces us to carry the weight of responsibility for shaping our own future. The choice to honor God, however, requires faith and trust. We hand control back to him; more importantly, we open our future to his possibilities. When we limit our future to what we can see, we may not get too excited. When we entrust our future to the potential that God sees, our possibilities are boundless.

The ambition of this world never breeds contentment. Honoring God won't ensure success, wealth, or renown. But we will be content. What a bonus!

Ambition at one time consumed the apostle Paul. He itemized his achievements in Philippians 3, then concluded:

> But whatever was to my profit I now consider loss
> for the sake of Christ. What is more, I consider
> everything a loss compared to the surpassing
> greatness of knowing Christ Jesus my Lord.... So,
> forgetting what is behind and straining toward
> what is ahead, I press on toward the goal to win
> the prize for which God has called me heavenward
> in Christ Jesus (3:7–8, 13–14).

Paul, in seeking to honor Christ above all else, knew Christ and gained the eternal prize. How strange that we become ambitious for temporary things and unconcerned about eternal things. God wants to correct our perspective.

The Costs

The countercultural way of God's kingdom does not make sense, especially to the person who places little stock in spiritual investment. Kingdom values differ so radically from our world that the moral digestive system of most people can't cope with them. This difference produces tension. Our natural side wants to believe it's possible for us to be ambitious but still utterly surrender to the will of the Lord. But Jesus spoke several times about the impossibility of equally serving two masters. One must prevail. We will either live for personal ambition or to honor God.

The costs of such countercultural choices include isolation from the mainstream. The decision to honor God above all else may mean a change of lifestyle; it will surely transform our life goals. Economics won't drive us; relationships will; not status, but humility; not power, but service. This will impact how we spend our time, how we allocate our resources, and how we treat others.

These changes will each certainly have a cost.

LIVING IT OUT

In October, 2002, former U.S. Senator for Kentucky Tim Philpot addressed a mayor's prayer breakfast in Fullerton, California, and described a meeting he had enjoyed several years earlier with Mother Teresa of Calcutta. This unassuming woman wanted only to honor Christ. Philpot at one point sat beside her and told her how he admired all she had done for the poor of India. He saw her ever so quickly raise her eyes and whisper the word "Jesus." If he had not been sitting within three feet of her, Philpot could not have heard what she said, but the stolen glance and the whispered word said it all.

God does not call all of us to take vows of poverty, but living his kingdom values will cause us more consistently to credit the Lord for every good thing in which we play a part. Rather than superspirituality or false humility, this expresses the heart that genuinely seeks to honor God after scoring a touchdown.

We struggle to apply this value. When we mix unhealthy doses of independence, competition, and ambition, we blend a potent cocktail that produces a destructive hangover. Seeking to honor God above ourselves goes against our natural grain. But that's what Paul meant when he spoke of being "transformed by the renewing of our minds" (Rom. 12:2).

Honoring God above all else has other implications for our lives, too. We will seek the Lord's leading in our lives rather than controlling and manipulating everything and everyone to achieve our goals. Again, we don't become utterly passive. We do, however, respond to the initiatives that God makes. We live each day seeking to grow more sensitive and responsive to his leading. We adopt an attentive posture: praying without ceasing, looking for evidence of God going before us, and listening to his Word.

In God's kingdom, we must replace personal ambition with a passionate and single-minded desire to serve and exalt God. Perhaps we will start each day by praying, "Lord, this is your day, not mine, to achieve your goals, not mine, to expand your kingdom, not mine. May everything I do bring honor to you. Amen."

150

Part Four

Attitudes Toward Life

.

Chapter Fourteen

What's the Score?

Success Clashes with Faithfulness

Mark Twain understood people. "Human nature is the same everywhere; it deifies success, it has nothing but scorn for defeat." As John Werkman detailed in his book *The American Paradox*, Americans push that drive for success to an extreme. Consider material prosperity as one of the forms of success in our culture.

Seventy-three percent of Americans entering college in the fall of 2001 ranked financial success as their primary goal. We Americans have, on the whole, attained that objective. Since 1960, per person income, adjusted for inflation, has more than tripled, from $6,000 to $20,000. We love our toys and comforts. But does this kind of success bring happiness?

Between 1960 and the early 1990s, the divorce rate has doubled; the teen suicide rate during that same period has tripled; reported violence has increased four times; the prison population has quintupled; the percentage of babies born to unmarried parents has increased sixfold. To what does Werkman attribute these failures?

Unbridled materialism. Financial success has not increased our happiness level. But what is success? Can we attain it? Does it work?

CULTURE'S VALUE

What It Is

We commonly define success as the favorable achievement of something we attempt or a goal we have. This definition highlights the two key elements—and the two key problems—with success as a driving value. First, achievement plays an innate role in success. Results enable us to keep score. The second difficulty deals with our choice of goals. Some goals possess merit, some don't. We may succeed in reaching our goal, only to find it doesn't satisfy us.

It's for Real

As Twain noted, we value success, and keeping score reveals our success, or its lack. Remember David's squash game with a friend in chapter 6? Keeping score was central to David's success over a rookie.

We build lists in order to quantify success. The Ten Richest People in America. The Twenty-five Fastest Growing Companies in America. Church seminars encourage leaders to establish quantifiable goals—so we can determine if we've succeeded.

As our success increases, so does our fame. The more fame, the more successful we seem to be. "Success," according to novelist Elias Canetti, "is the space one occupies in the newspaper." How many of us have searched the Internet to see if our names appear? We yearn to validate our lives by claiming our "fifteen minutes of fame."

Success for others means having enough to waste or to be extravagant. Barbra Streisand has said, "Success to me is having ten honeydew melons and eating only the top half of each one." Whether money, cars, or honeydews, we often measure success by excess.

We tend to feel successful if we perform better than someone else or if we hold down a better-paying job or occupy a more important position. Novelist Ursula Le Guin claims, "Success is somebody else's failure." Of course, we must be careful to whom we compare ourselves! Depending on whom we pick, we can just as easily come out behind.

Finally, physical attractiveness consistently correlates with success. "In my time and neighborhood (and in my soul)," author Jessamyn West proclaims, "there was only one standard by which a woman measured success: did some man want her?" Attractive people receive promotions more than the unattractive; tall people tend to get elected to "higher" office.

The Payoffs

Establishing goals allows us to define success. As we set targets, we know how to guide our lives. Keeping score then allows us to determine success. We can determine our progress in the pursuit of success. The university where David and Tim teach has an online component to the courses— students can access their current grades at any time. They can measure their success whenever they wish.

Having clear goals and measurable standards brings personal satisfaction. When we reach our goals, we feel successful. Rocker John Otway says, "There's no point in success if you don't let it go to your head. That's what it's for." Success feeds our ego. We feel important and significant.

The Costs

But success *doesn't always satisfy*. The statistics we cited from Werkman indicate that reaching our goals may not increase happiness. Emptiness seems actually to increase when the goals for which we've worked don't satisfy us. We then have little left.

More significantly, the goals and standards we choose for success *may work against spiritual well-being*. Think about the goals by which our culture defines success: fame, popularity, material goods, career advancement, and physical attractiveness. God commends none of these as attributes of success. The biblical evidence indicates that, rather than helping our spiritual search, they may instead hinder it.

GOD'S VALUE

What It Is

In opposition to our culture's deification of goal setting and score keeping, God advocates faithfulness. We are to do our best to seek after what God desires, then leave the results in God's domain. In fact, the words "succeed" and "success" do not even occur in the New Testament.

Mother Teresa expressed it well when she said, "I do not pray for success. I ask for faithfulness."

It's for Real

Achievement lies at the heart of our culture's concept of success. But we can't guarantee results, regardless of how hard we work or the talents and education we possess. We can do our best and still not achieve success from the world's viewpoint. Just think of the cultural standards of success we cited earlier. We won't *all* gain fame; neither will we all accumulate material goods. We may be more apt, compared to others, to come in second place. In fact, when we compare ourselves against each other, we miss the kingdom value completely. The apostle Paul wrote, "When they measure themselves by themselves and compare themselves with themselves, they are without understanding" (2 Cor. 10:12 NASB).

Even spiritual results lie outside our control. "I planted the seed, Apollos watered it, but God made it grow. So neither he who plants nor he who waters is anything, but only God, who makes things grow" (1 Cor. 3:6–7).

Instead of continually driving for the big numbers, however, God expects us to be faithful. Saul seemed successful as the first king of Israel. He had fame, material goods, and he was physically attractive. He achieved much, particularly in 1 Samuel 15. God told Saul to lead a war against the Amalekites and to totally destroy everything. Saul achieved victory in the battle, but he kept some of the best flocks and herds. He told Samuel the prophet that he had kept them in order to sacrifice them to God.

God didn't value Saul's success the way Saul did. "Does the

LORD delight in burnt offerings and sacrifices as much as in obeying the voice of the LORD? To obey is better than sacrifice ..." (15:22).

That episode marked the turning point in Saul's reign. It began to tumble downhill. God wants faithfulness, not success. Faithfulness means we focus on doing what God wants us to do. Hebrews 3:1–2, 6 highlights this for us:

> Therefore, holy brothers, who share in the
> heavenly calling, fix your thoughts on Jesus, the
> apostle and high priest whom we confess. He was
> faithful to the one who appointed him, just as
> Moses was faithful in all God's house ... . But
> Christ is faithful as a son over God's house. And
> we are his house, if we hold on to our courage and
> the hope of which we boast.

We will counter our culture's stress on success and achievement as we courageously and faithfully obey God.

The Payoffs

First, when we accept God's value of faithfulness, we *redefine what matters most* in life. Fame and other cultural successes may escape our grasp, but every follower of Jesus can be faithful. The apostle Paul clarified our responsibilities. We plant or water to the best of our ability, and that matters to God. Why? God bears the responsibility for the results of our actions.

Second, *God delights in our faithful obedience* and gives us greater intimacy with him. The success of this world doesn't last. Faithfulness yields eternal fruit, especially the pleasure of God.

The Costs

Obedience, however, will clearly cost us, since it leads us to the *sacrifice of our own desires*. Our desires will yield to God's. Saul failed spiritually when he valued the spoils of war over God's command to destroy everything. Obedience would have eliminated gaining the rewards of war.

Faithfulness can also lead to *loss of comfort, ease, money, and even life*. Martin Burnham of New Tribes Mission in the Philippines was faithful to God, but his obedience required him to pay a high cost. He was kidnapped in May 2001 by Muslim extremists. He lost his life a year later in a June 2002 rescue attempt. We can easily argue that he gained something greater, but we cannot escape the truth that he lost his life. His wife lost her husband; their children lost their father.

LIVING IT OUT

Way back at the age of twenty-four, I (Tim) sensed a tug toward youth ministry. I prayed, pondered, and sought advice. One major fear remained. What if I couldn't hack it? What if I wasn't successful? What if my youth group didn't reach new young people? What if it didn't grow?

I then found 1 Corinthians 3:6–7 and learned that results weren't up to me. My task was simply to do my best at what God wanted me to do and then leave the rest to God. That opened the door to what became a fruitful youth work and decades in various forms of ministry.

I discovered four steps to faithfulness. First, we *value obedience*. Place obedience above achievement, goals, and scorekeeping. God's commands may not always make sense. They may conflict with our own desires, and they may have a significant cost. Obedience to them may put us at odds with society. But we believe the Father knows best.

Second, we *do our job*. Whatever God calls us to do, we do it with gusto. Be fully engaged. Whether your ministry is upfront or backstage, just do it.

Third, we *take risks*. I (Tim) discovered the freedom that comes from giving up responsibility for results. We'll attempt difficult tasks that we'd otherwise avoid. My new endeavors of college teaching and professional writing have each involved more risk than the "safe" local church ministry in which I'd been for decades. But the risk was worth it.

Fourth, we *embrace failure*. Risk increases our failure rate. Not all colleges wanted to hire me. Not every publisher wanted to publish my work. But faithfulness provides the courage to risk failure. We can learn from it, if only in knowing what to avoid in the future. God tends to use failure more than "success" to shape us.

I (David) have had these lessons reinforced over the years, too. As a church planter, I felt great pressure to "succeed." By many standards, I did. But who sets those standards? Too often, our church culture, not God, does. I came to realize that God did not call me to succeed in just one area of life but to be faithful in every area—marriage, family, and friendship as well as church. This calling demands more of us, but it also frees us.

In a world that emphasizes goals, scorekeeping, and achievement, we hold to a far greater value—faithfulness to God.

Chapter Fifteen

Show Me the Money!

Accumulation Clashes with Giving

Mix together a top-ranked daily cable news show, gobs of merchandising, several best-selling books, and a radio show. The result? The fast-rising Bill O'Reilly of Fox News. And along with Bill comes a large income. He won't reveal how large, just that it is, indeed, large.

Next comes the surprise. In his book *The O'Reilly Factor*, he reveals that he drives a used car and wouldn't consider buying a cup of Starbucks coffee. Not that he dislikes the brew. And he can certainly afford it. He just thinks they charge too much for it at $3.50 per latte. Refills extra. He doesn't buy jewelry and even avoids facing the spending temptations of Home Depot.

What does O'Reilly do with the money he makes and saves? Store it up for an early retirement with a motor home? Secure his family's financial security? Rather than accumulating it, he gives away much of it.

What an odd man! In a culture that values making and accumulating money, O'Reilly stands in the company of a small group.

CULTURE'S VALUE

What It Is

Our culture values money. Making it. Spending it. Particularly, accumulating it. A new book, *The Millionaire Next Door*, claims that almost any American can accumulate a million dollars. Our culture places a high value on such accumulation.

We honor Bill Gates, the wealthiest man in America. If he stopped just long enough to pick up a $100 bill off the ground, he would lose money in the time he used. We would without hesitation pick it up!

It's for Real

Accumulation of money, property, and possessions permeates our culture. We've all laughed at the bumper sticker, "He who dies with the most toys wins." Movies express that value. What line from *Jerry McGuire* has become infamous? "Show me the money!" Don't *talk* about getting me money; *get it*!

Gordon Gecko in the 1987 movie *Wall Street* proclaimed, "Greed is good. Greed works. Greed is right ... and greed, mark my words, will save not only Teldar Paper but the other malfunctioning corporation called the USA."

We might question that now, with the many corporate scandals that have rocked our nation's economy.

Professional athletes will leave a team where they make "only" $5 million a year in order to pull down $20 million with another. Their rationale? "I just want to assure my family's financial security." All of us could be quite secure on much less than $5 million per year.

This malady doesn't afflict just the wealthy; it seems we all want to accumulate. "Normal" guys accumulate tools and toys; "normal" women accumulate jewelry and clothes.

The Payoffs

How do we benefit from this accumulation? We *increase our financial security*. Our savings and retirement accounts grow and we rest easier at the prospect of comfortable retirement years.

We *grow in self-esteem*. We feel important when we make money. We feel more successful than Joe when we discover we make more than he does. While our net worth doesn't give us personal value, we tend to think otherwise.

We *enjoy the benefits of material wealth* and accumulation: more toys, higher technology, and nicer stuff. We all enjoy acquiring a new high-speed computer, the surround sound system, and the latest model car.

The Costs

When we devote our lives to accumulation, *strained relationships* lead the list of the costs. Couples who both work long hours to afford the cars, the house, the clothing, and the toys commonly find they sacrifice both marriage and children. A more extreme example highlights the point. The drug lords of Mexico have in recent years been found dead—killed by the enemies they made in the pursuit of wealth. Their devotion to accumulation eliminated safe relationships and ultimately cost them their lives.

Monetary success can be addictive. Bill O'Reilly commented in his book, "Here's something that really surprises me: the more stuff I have, the more stuff I want. And so I looked around and saw everyone was the same way. It was not until I had a few things that I noticed how this works. The material stuff is addicting!"

Why? Because money by itself cannot satisfy. Stories tell of an interviewer who asked J. Paul Getty, at one time the richest man alive, how much money it would take to satisfy him. He thought for a second and replied, "Just a little more."

Another cost reveals the most serious flaw: *we trust in wealth*, not God. Jesus told in Luke 12 of a man who trusted in his accumulated wealth and took steps to increase it even more. He died unfulfilled, and Jesus concluded, "This is how it will be with anyone who stores up things for himself but is not rich toward God" (v. 21).

GOD'S VALUE

What It Is

Followers of Jesus discover dueling values when it comes to money. Our culture values the accumulation of it for predominantly personal uses or to demonstrate our success. God values money only as a tool to meet both our own and others' personal needs. Jesus explained the difference in Matthew 6:19–21, 24.

Do not store up for yourselves treasures on earth, where moth and rust destroy, and where thieves break in and steal. But store up for yourselves treasures in heaven, where moth and rust do not destroy, and where thieves do not break in and steal. For where your treasure is, there your heart will be also. ... No one can serve two masters. Either he will hate the one and love the other, or he will be devoted to the one and despise the other. You cannot serve both God and Money.

Our culture values accumulating money; God values the wise and generous giving of it.

It's for Real

God's view of wealth involves two elements: source and purpose.

We adopt God's perspective when we understand that he is the source and owner of all material things. Psalm 24:1–2 presents a radical principle, "The earth is the LORD'S, and everything in it, the world, and all who live in it; for he founded it upon the seas and established it upon the waters."

We don't *own*; we just have it on *loan*. God retains ownership even as he provides things for our use.

Second, "God the Owner" has established several purposes for having and using wealth. Wealth exists first to meet our needs. Second Corinthians 9:10 tells us, "Now he who supplies seed to the sower and bread for food will also supply and increase your store of seed and will enlarge the harvest of your righteousness." God knows we have physical needs and he provides for them.

Wealth, according to the verses that immediately follow the passage above, exists secondly to meet the needs of others: "This service that you perform is … supplying the needs of God's people …" As we receive material wealth, we allow God's love to flow through us and use it to help those in need.

The third use of wealth finds its basis in the familiar Matthew 6:20 passage: "But store up for yourselves treasures in heaven, where moth and rust do not destroy, and where thieves do not break in and steal."

We build a savings account with God as we use earthly wealth for heavenly purposes. God provides wealth so that we can use it to bring others to him. Surprise! As we invest resources in people by our generous giving, we *can* take it with us!

The Payoffs

As we learn to give, we discover an effective cure for greed. Giving attacks our desire to accumulate. We fight the tendency as we give, and learn that we can survive.

Giving both expresses and builds faith. We can't give sacrificially until we trust in God. A group of Christians from Macedonia in the first century gave sacrificially, but it came from their faith and further strengthened their faith. "They did not do as we expected, but they gave themselves first to the Lord and then to us in keeping with God's will" (2 Cor. 8:5).

The more we give out of faith, the more like God we become. But downsides also exist when we reject accumulation and embrace giving.

The Costs

Obviously, we tend to have *less money* when we give away wealth! Sacrificial giving requires our spending and accumulation habits to change. Giving to benefit others and the kingdom of God decreases the amount of money available to us.

Because of that, we may seem to have *less financial security*. Since accumulating wealth brings a sense of security, when we decrease our accumulation, we decrease our reliance on wealth for that well-being and comfort. Giving then becomes an expression of our faith and trust in God, our ultimate security.

LIVING IT OUT

We can make three adjustments to counter our culture's focus on accumulating wealth.

First, *adopt a manager's attitude*. We should always remember that God owns everything. As we evaluate financial options, let's think of ways to use what we have for the honor of the Owner, not to accumulate for ourselves.

Second, *adopt a generous and joyful attitude*. For too many Christians, giving is a distasteful duty. We give out of obligation, guilt, or to secure God's blessing. But as Paul wrote in 2 Corinthians 9:6–7, "Remember this: Whoever sows sparingly will also reap sparingly, and whoever sows generously will also reap generously. Each man should give what he has decided in his heart to give, not reluctantly or under compulsion, for God loves a cheerful giver." Of course, as someone has quipped, "God *loves* a cheerful giver, but he *accepts* from grouches."

Let's not be stingy and carefully monitor our giving. God will bless us generously as we generously give. And let's give cheerfully. The Greek word for "cheerful" provides the root for the English word "hilarious." Give hilariously. Laugh as you give. Roll in the aisles. Let your giving be an excited contrast to the culture's value of accumulation.

Third, *adopt a sacrificial attitude.* God gave his Son as a sacrifice for us and as a pattern for us to copy. This leads to one of the most difficult applications.

We believe in giving 10 percent of our income as the starting point for our giving. We call that tithing. For many of us, especially when we begin, that represents a sacrifice. But once we've tithed for some time, we adjust. God blesses us, we prosper, and we may never even notice the absence of the 10 percent. We think God desires, not equal giving, but equal sacrifice. So as we grow in generosity, God may call us to move beyond *proportional* giving to *sacrificial* giving.

Let's be sacrificial. Like God. Like the churches in Macedonia.

> And now, brothers, we want you to know about the grace that God has given the Macedonian churches. Out of the most severe trial, their overflowing joy and their extreme poverty welled up in rich generosity. For I testify that they gave as much as they were able, and even *beyond their ability.* Entirely on their own, they urgently pleaded with us for the privilege of … [giving] to the saints (2 Cor. 8:1–4, emphasis added).

Sacrificial giving may best represent how we counter our culture's value of accumulation. When we practice it, our lives change.

Tim's wife, Sheila, had just come back to God and church while still a single mother. Every penny of income had a corresponding expense. Then the pastor visited and taught about Christian giving. Sheila quickly realized the conflict. Yes, tithing was important; no, she wasn't practicing it; neither could she afford to. But God said it.

The next Sunday as she wrote a check for 10 percent of that week's income, a strange combination of joy and fear ran through her heart. Joy from obeying; fear from not knowing how the budget would balance. The next day at work, her boss called her in. "Sheila, we appreciate the good work you've been doing. We'd like to give you a raise, effective this week." The amount of the raise matched the difference between her small previous giving and the recent tithe.

God honored her giving. It proved far better than accumulation.

David and his wife, Kim, recently learned to deal with the culture's value when they gave their nearly new garden shed to their neighbors. They intentionally did so to minimize their capacity to accumulate. But it also has opened doors to share their lives and God's love with the neighbors. When you give something away, it loses its hold on you. And this leads us deeper into kingdom living.

Chapter Sixteen

One for the Road

Consumerism Clashes with Simplicity

True story. John and Ruth headed out in their well-used Volvo from Southern California for a vacation in the Midwest. Although Volvos of that vintage have rarely impressed people with their styling or performance, they've earned their reputation for reliability and safety. But even well-engineered machines wear out, and a slight mechanical problem forced the couple to layover in Las Vegas for repairs.

They took advantage of a nearby casino's inexpensive meals, and on their way out Ruth took a few quarters of the change from lunch and "invested" them in a slot machine. All the bells and whistles in the world went off; she'd hit the jackpot and won a brand new Corvette.

Rather than driving off with the new 'Vette and impressing their family and friends with that slick speed-machine, they traded it in for a new Volvo and gave the old one to a young minister with a family. When someone asked John why, he replied, "I guess we're just not Corvette people."

Sean approached his windfall differently. He received an unexpected promotion at his software company that doubled his income. His family of just three soon drove around in a loaded Ford Expedition while he tooled around in a Mustang GT convertible. They moved into a custom home, and the number and extravagant nature of their toys increased even as they continued to give generously to their church.

Why did both of these families respond as differently as they did? They had very different views on the use of resources.

CULTURE'S VALUE

What It Is

Consumerism transcends materialism, which focuses on things. It also goes beyond accumulation, the desire to have *more* things. Consumerism *uses* things. It spends, exploits, and devours. The consumer lifestyle uses, discards, and wastes.

Tell most people in our high-consumption culture to cut back the number of products they buy or to reuse things multiple times or to buy a Ford instead of the Lexus they can afford, and just watch their reaction. The "right" to consume has embedded itself in us as a core value.

It's for Real

Take a short walk down the aisles of a grocery store. Count the number of different breakfast cereals and cookie products.

Consider the many recycling programs we have enacted to deal with the staggeringly high volume of containers and wrappers we discard. When did you last walk half a mile for anything other than exercise? We all jump in the car but hesitate to carpool. We want to drive *our* car. Carpool lanes on freeways are lonely places, especially in Southern California.

We no longer wash diapers but buy disposable ones. We prefer new furniture to used. We constantly add to our wardrobe despite the good condition of the clothing we already have.

The Brandt Commission issued a report twenty years ago noting that 20 percent of the world's population consumes 80 percent of the world's resources. The U.S. alone—with just 6 percent of the world's population—uses 40 percent of the resources.

Our culture loves to upgrade, improve, use, and discard. Most companies now build machinery with obsolescence in mind. They *want* our household appliances to break down within three to five years, forcing us to buy more.

We want faster, more powerful computers, although most of us can't fully utilize the capabilities of the machines we already have. Consider the number of restaurant and fast food meals you have eaten this past month. I (David) recall the treat of three visits over the course of a year to Kentucky Fried Chicken when I was a teenager in the 1970s. Many families today think nothing of eating out three times a week.

Our cars have increased in both complexity and luxury. Features such as power windows, remote locking devices, CD stacks, and cruise control either didn't exist twenty years ago or were uncommon options. Now we can't imagine driving without them.

I (Tim) grew up in the 1950s in a typical three-bedroom, one-bath home that totaled 1200 square feet. Nearly unimaginable today. Weddings have moved beyond the simple ceremony, often conducted in the pastor's home, to become elaborate and expensive productions. High school proms commonly involve not only rented tuxedos and expensive dresses but stretch limousines with hot tubs—all for a single evening's entertainment.

The list goes on. Our culture not only consumes a lot of resources but also revels in using unnecessary and extravagant items.

The Payoffs

Convenience may head the list of benefits. Organizing a carpool takes time and effort—and then we can't always listen to *our* CDs or favorite radio station. Rather than plan and cook a meal after work, we stop for fast food. A bedroom for everyone sure beats sharing a room.

Consumerism pays off in terms of *comfort*. Who wants to run a fan if we can enjoy air conditioning? We prefer staying in a three-star hotel over camping. A hot shower running over our tired body for twenty minutes feels better than a quick three-minute run-through.

Consumerism brings *more pleasure*. Why drink water if we can get free refills of Coke from the waitress? Why not try a bit of everything at the buffet table, even if it takes three plates to carry it back to the table? It surely tastes good, even if we have to starve ourselves for two days to unload the excess calories.

And it is no wonder that we consume so heavily; we have the financial resources.

The Costs

Heavy personal, social, and global costs accompany consumerism. They include obesity, poor health, and lower productivity. Our overconsumption of food, beverages, and pharmaceuticals, for example, hardly makes us healthy individuals. Some of our momentary pleasures produce frustrating obstacles to our long-term well-being.

Consumerism also *negatively impacts society*. Pollution and waste disposal choke our cities with smog, fill our rivers with garbage, and destroy our fisheries with chemicals.

The demand of Western consumers for cheaper products results in the exploitation of sweat-shop labor in Third World countries. Our extravagance and waste in the West would more than cover the needs of many of the hungry and homeless around the world. We instead consume it ourselves, and we've created no mechanism to capture the excess and to funnel it to those who need help.

GOD'S VALUE

What It Is

The kingdom of God, in contrast to consumerism, values simplicity. A simple lifestyle. Such a concept goes beyond just giving and sharing. It happens when we choose to live simply so that others may simply live. We decide to reduce consumption, specifically so that others may share the abundance with which God has blessed us.

It's for Real

We can trace this theme of simplicity throughout the Bible. When the Jews wandered in the wilderness for forty years, God daily provided the simple food of manna for them to eat. But they soon grew bored with the flakes that tasted like honey and olive oil, and requested a more extensive menu. So God brought quail, which they overate. They then experienced a plague. (Perhaps you have occasionally felt that way after one of those all-you-can-eat buffets.) God wasn't pleased with their lack of contentment with a simple meal (see Num. 11).

Jesus taught us to focus not on earthly, but rather on heavenly, treasures (see Matt. 6:19–20). We are not to allow our consumerism to override a simple life that makes room for God. A Jewish lawyer on one occasion came to Jesus and expressed the desire to follow him. Jesus replied, "The foxes have holes and the birds of the air have nests; but the Son of Man has nowhere to lay his head" (Matt. 8:20 NASB). Jesus doubted that the lawyer would follow him because doing so required a radically simple lifestyle.

A wealthy man came on another occasion to Jesus and asked what he should do to find eternal life. The reply? "'If you wish to be complete, go and sell your possessions and give to the poor, and you will have treasure in heaven.' The young man went away grieved because he owned a lot of property" (Matt. 19:21–22 NASB). What a tough teaching! Jesus challenged him not to allow consumption to get in the way of following. Instead, he was to live more simply.

Of course, Jesus himself modeled this. The apostle Paul wrote that, although Jesus existed in the form of God, he emptied himself, taking the form of a servant to accomplish the redemptive plan of God (see Phil. 2:6–7). This doesn't mean that all of us should live like servants or sell everything we have and give it to the poor. Simplicity expresses an attitude and doesn't make a statement of our wealth. Even a dirt-poor person may not embrace simplicity. We may sell everything but still at heart be wasteful consumers. Conversely, we may have considerable resources, as Bill O'Reilly does (see chapter 15), yet still embrace simplicity.

This raises an important biblical teaching about contentment. The apostle Paul told Timothy that "Godliness with contentment is great gain" (1 Tim. 6:6). He testified earlier,

> I have learned to be content whatever the
> circumstances. I know what it is to be in need, and
> I know what it is to have plenty. I have learned the
> secret of being content in any and every situation,
> whether well fed or hungry, whether living in
> plenty or in want. I can do everything through
> him who gives me strength (Phil. 4:11–13).

Paul's secret to contentment was trusting Christ in everything. Without the critical component of contentment, we will practice simplicity grudgingly. With contentment, however, we will do it with joy. Without it, simplicity is merely an outward action; with it, a statement of the heart.

Again, we choose to live simply that others may simply live. This approach to life produces remarkable dividends.

The Payoffs

First, it allows us *to make genuine provision for others* in this world. I (Tim) once faced a haunting choice. I had an opportunity to buy a high-priced sports car. My current car satisfied my needs; the new car would satisfy my yearnings. But the new car would have decreased my ability to help support an orphanage in Tijuana, Mexico. The home gets children off the streets, has brought hundreds to Christ over the years, and has challenged many to serve Christ. The Mexican orphanage won. Simplicity can make this kind of difference in the world.

Simplicity also *protects us against the subtle stranglehold of consumerism.* Only when we give away what we hold do we break the hold of what we have. The decision to live more simply strikes a blow that frees us from materialism and consumerism.

Furthermore, our choice to live more simply *empowers our witness* and opens doors for sharing our faith. The first church in Jerusalem decided that all things would be common property among them (see Acts 4:32–37 NASB). People did not claim anything for themselves. The group chose to live simply. Verse 33 tells us that their witness was with great power and "abundant grace was upon them all." Did one cause the other? We perhaps need to think about that.

Finally, simplicity accompanied by contentment *produces a stronger faith* and a richer relationship with God. After all, if we live at the very center of his will, we live in the very best place.

The Costs

A decision to live simply has some obvious costs. Our inventory of possessions will certainly change because the choice to live simply touches the issue of accumulation. If we live simply so that we can give to others, we will also obviously spend less on ourselves.

Perhaps our lifestyles will change the most. Issues of convenience, comfort, and pleasure will require a fresh evaluation. When we choose to change our habits of consuming, we'll face inconvenience. A family with two shared vehicles among four drivers will need to negotiate and plan ahead more than before. The all-you-can-eat buffet won't be as frequent a restaurant choice. Television viewing habits will change once we cancel our cable subscription.

We each need to consider how simply we will live, and our decision will have different ramifications for each of us. Change and adjustment rarely come easily.

LIVING IT OUT

Michael Grosso, in his book *The Millennial Myth*, states, "The American dream has evolved from a puritanical frugality to pagan consumerism." Both extremes offer problems. And we certainly do not endorse puritanical frugality as the alternative to consumerism.

Andrew Carnegie, the American steel magnate who accumulated an estate of over $250 million by 1901, understood the temptation of extravagant consumerism.

> This, then, is held to be the duty of the man of wealth: First, to set an example of modest, unostentatious living, shunning display or extravagance; to provide moderately for the legitimate wants of those dependent upon him; and, after doing so, to consider all surplus revenues which come to him simply as trust funds, which he is called upon to administer, and strictly bound as a matter of duty to administer in the manner which, in his judgment, is best calculated to produce the most beneficial results for the community—the man of wealth thus becoming the mere trustee and agent....

Richard Foster, in his book *Freedom of Simplicity*, shares an illustration of the power of this kingdom value.

> As Hudson Taylor prepared to bring the Gospel to the great throngs of inland China, he taught himself to endure hardship and to economize in order to help people in need. He said, "I soon found that I could live upon very much less than I had previously thought possible. Butter, milk, and other luxuries I ceased to use, and found that by living mainly on oatmeal and rice, with occasional variations, a very small sum was sufficient for my

needs." In this way, he was able to use two-thirds of his income for other purposes. He wrote: "My experience was that the less I spent on myself and the more I gave to others, the fuller of happiness and blessing did my soul become."

We do not recommend that everyone live on oatmeal and rice. The lesson from Hudson Taylor is this: As he reduced what he consumed, he found that he could reach far more people than he had imagined. Imagine what might happen if believers decided to reject consumerism and embrace simpler lifestyles for the Gospel.

I'll Get to It When I Get to It

Laziness Clashes with Diligence

The turbulent 60s and early 70s influenced many people, including me (Tim). I finished my bachelor's degree at Pepperdine University in 1970 and entered the master's degree program in Communications. I completed all the classes, the oral examination, and did the research for my thesis. I then lost focus.

I had no specific career plans for a graduate degree. So, following the spirit of those days, I let things "drift." I never chose not to *finish* it; neither did I choose to *complete* it. My mom thought I was lazy. I think in retrospect she was right.

But the lack of a master's degree never seemed to be a problem. I spent time in business, reentered the pastoral ministry, and served in several churches. During a trip to my much-loved Sierra Nevada Mountains, a long-time friend suggested that I consider teaching at Hope International

University, a Christian school. The position matched my gifts and interests, particularly with the friend serving on the board of directors there. I made an appointment to discuss the opportunity with the president. The lack of a graduate degree immediately became a problem.

My laziness with the master's degree took thirty years to become an issue. How much better to have been diligent thirty years earlier! Our culture often encourages laziness. Not necessarily doing nothing, but not being diligent.

CULTURE'S VALUE

What It Is

Most of us, when the subject of laziness arises, think it doesn't apply to us. We work. We're active. We achieve. Rather than "just doing nothing," however, laziness can involve working at a low intensity. *Webster's Dictionary* defines *lazy* as "disinclined to activity or exertion; not energetic or vigorous; encouraging inactivity or indolence; to move slowly."

Laziness can involve doing the bare minimum; that matches our typical perception. But it also includes a lack of self-exertion. We move, but slowly. We work, but not energetically. We don't put our full effort into the task. We do enough to make ourselves feel good, enough to cover the basics, but we don't extend ourselves.

It's for Real

Years ago, George Robeson wrote a column in the Long Beach *Independent Press Telegram* in which he bemoaned the loss of his greatest excuse. When his wife asked him to do a task, he'd reply, "When I get around to it." He just never got around to it! One day, she gave him a circular disc with the letters "TUIT" on the surface. He lost his laziness rationale when he received a round "tuit." Many of us need to get "a round tuit" for a variety of tasks.

Laziness touches our culture in many ways. School test scores have plummeted in America, and many students enter college academically under prepared. One reason: the lack of industriousness on the part of parents, teachers, and students. Many companies suffer from low productivity and small profits. One reason: lack of diligence by management and workers. Churches survive, but few succeed at reaching the unchurched. One reason: lack of earnest biblical goal setting for the church.

Each of these symptoms reflects the problem of laziness in our society. It's not that we do nothing; we just don't give it our all. We lack diligence. The proliferation of laziness in home, school, and industry indicates this has become a core value for many people.

The Payoffs

But amazingly, laziness actually *works* for us! First, it yields *an easy life*. We don't drive ourselves, so we move at a more relaxed pace. Laziness allows us to find a comfort zone and to *stay* there. No challenges. No changes. Few demands. An easy life. Or so we think.

Second, we may have *less stress*. By lowering our expectations, we lower our frustrations. When we care deeply about achieving something and don't succeed, we experience disappointment and stress. If we, therefore, decide it doesn't really matter, our stress level goes down.

Third, laziness can serve as a means of *gaining control* of our lives. Another person may ask us to do something, and we find it difficult to say no. We dislike others telling us what to do, so we just procrastinate, go slow, and dawdle. Laziness kicks in as a strategy for maintaining control of our lives.

The Costs

But laziness also damages us. It often leads to a *lower standard of living*. When we don't put as much effort into life, we receive less out of it. "Lazy hands make a man poor, but diligent hands bring wealth" (Prov. 10:4).

We don't suggest that all poverty results from laziness, but *some* of it does. The diligence a good education requires produces a payoff in the form of higher income. Laziness in the workplace frequently robs us of promotions and salary increases. Supervisors rarely reward lazy workers.

Laziness frequently leads to the *decay of material goods*. A good friend of Tim's works hard at yard work. But when the job is done, he's done, often leaving behind his tools to rust. He seems forever to be purchasing replacements. If we get lazy about changing the oil and maintaining the fluid levels in our car, we will soon experience a breakdown. Ecclesiastes 10:18 states, "If a man is lazy, the rafters sag; if his hands are idle, the house leaks."

Finally, the "easy life" *minimizes personal growth*. Growth results from activity, not dormancy. The oft-told story of the kind-hearted kid who snipped off the end of the cocoon to make it easy for the butterfly to come out illustrates this reality. The effort required to break through a cocoon and to squeeze through a small opening pumps blood into the butterfly's wings, enabling it to live and fly. The young boy meant to help but managed, instead, to kill the butterfly. Elimination of the need for exertion may hurt more than it helps.

GOD'S VALUE

What It Is

In contrast to the tendency toward laziness we see in our culture, God encourages diligence. *Webster's Dictionary* defines diligence as, "characterized by steady, earnest, and energetic application and effort; to persevere."

Three passages in Proverbs contrast diligence with laziness (see 10:4; 12:24, 27). Diligence suggests that we energetically work toward a goal. We don't get sidetracked as I (Tim) did with my master's degree at Pepperdine. I put in my time but didn't persevere in the program.

It's for Real

Biblical diligence has two dimensions.

First, we work purposefully. We choose a goal and work to reach it. We find a great example in the story in Matthew 25:14–27 that Jesus told. A well-off employer gave one employee $5,000 to invest; to another, he gave $2,000; and to a third, $1,000. The goal was to multiply the money for the employer. The first worker went right to work, as did the second. They both doubled what they had received and demonstrated diligence. The third just rat-holed the money. Safe, secure, buried in the ground. No chance of losing it. No chance of increasing it.

The employer later returned and asked the employees to account for how they used his money. He praised and rewarded the first two but condemned the third. Why?

> You wicked, *lazy* servant! So you knew that I harvest where I have not sown and gather where I have not scattered seed? Well then, you should have put my money on deposit with the bankers, so that when I returned I would have received it back with interest. … And throw that worthless servant outside, into the darkness, where there will be weeping and gnashing of teeth (Matt. 25:26–27, 30, emphasis added).

The first two had a clear goal and worked earnestly toward it. We call that diligence. The third did nothing. We call that laziness. Remember, laziness may not necessarily be the absence of work, but the lack of *vigorous* and *purposeful* labor.

But rather than focus on drivenness and ceaseless toil, biblical diligence also includes the discipline of rest. We take breaks. Recreate. Worship. Occasionally sit and purposefully do nothing. God, when he created the world, stopped, rested, and enjoyed it. God, when he began a covenant relationship with people, commanded that they stop and take a break. Jesus, when engulfed by the stress of meeting people's needs, paused and took breaks. Ought we not today to follow God's example?

Diligence does not require uninterrupted work, constantly moving at full speed. We need to sleep. We need to connect with others and to play. We need to slow down in order to think, to evaluate, to enjoy leisure activities, and to invest time together in community.

The greatest laziness of our day may be in the area of building relationships. The workaholic who puts in seventy hours per week and the stay-at-home mom who incessantly cleans the house may display the wrong kind of diligence. Biblical diligence encompasses *all* of life. Our lives, in addition to building our careers, include the roles of spouse, parent, and grandparent. Serving Christ in the church is just as important as serving our employer. Indeed, if we focus exclusively on just one area, we may inadvertently become lazy in the more comprehensive journey of life.

The Payoffs

The greatest advantage of diligence lies in our *usefulness to God*. The first two workers in the Matthew 25 story advanced the cause of their employer. When we act diligently, God honors us by using us.

Second, when we avoid laziness we more effectively *meet material needs*. We establish a goal to gain the needed stuff of life. We do what's necessary to reach it. We often reach our goal. We might not become rich, but neither do we starve. "If anyone will not work," Paul wrote, "neither let him eat" (2 Thess. 3:10 ASV).

Third, *we live life more fully*. We choose a direction in life and craft our activities to arrive at a particular destination.

And part of life's fullness stems from the purpose that guides our lives. Diligent lives have purpose and focus.

Last, we build *appropriate self-esteem*. Galatians 6:4 says, "Each one should test his own actions. Then he can take pride in himself, without comparing himself to somebody else." Regularly check out your activities. Do you have goals? Do you work effectively to reach them? Are you pausing for breaks? Biblical diligence satisfies.

The Costs

Diligence at the same time carries a price tag. First, it requires us to become *more intentional* about our life direction and the contribution we can make to others. Rather than "taking life as it comes," we need to think, pray, study, evaluate, and choose goals. We must then determine the most effective ways to reach those goals. This can be difficult work for many of us!

Second, we *work harder.* Diligence demands energy. We must manage our time differently so we can work more diligently in multiple areas of our lives and less obsessively in just one or two areas. The increased energy-demands may require us to modify our exercise and eating routines.

This new way of living will impact whatever demands most of our time now. Some of us will need to give up our favorite television programming. Others among us will have to reduce our working hours. Still others may need to spend less time on the golf course. The required changes will be different for each of us. Whatever those changes might be, the requirements of biblical diligence will surprise us.

LIVING IT OUT

In order to live out God's value of diligence, we need to remember God's definition: purposeful effort. We must first *set goals*. The owner in the story Jesus told commissioned the three workers to use the owner's money for the owner's benefit. Since our lives as Christians belong to God, we must likewise establish directions for our lives that aim to benefit God, others, and then ourselves.

But we also need to *work well*. That means we don't dread work but cherish it as a tool to accomplish God's purposes and to give significance to our lives. My (Tim's) wife, Sheila, recently felt frustrated that the at-home jobs didn't seem to be getting done. So we sat down and developed a "honey-do" list that totaled thirty-five items. I felt even better than Sheila as we completed each item on the list.

We can sometimes work hard but end up spreading ourselves too thin on too many tasks, so pick the most important ones. Then work diligently to finish them.

Third, *take breaks*. Diligence doesn't mean that *all* we do is work! God established and commanded a day of rest. Jesus frequently took time out from crucial ministry. God designed our bodies, minds, and spirits to take breaks. A good night of sleep. A day of worship and relaxation each week. Smaller breaks during the day. These allow us to work more diligently.

Remember my (Tim's) laziness at completing my Master of Arts at Pepperdine? I'm slowly learning. Since then, I've completed a master's degree in ministry. I even took the humbling step of applying to Pepperdine for readmission to the master's in Communication program. I'm now pursuing that and am considering applying for a Ph.D. program to enhance my university teaching. I've made the commitment to be more diligent.

Whereas Tim has been learning some important lessons, I (David) find professional diligence fairly easy since I enjoy my work. But diligence in relationships provides a challenge for me. I tend to immerse myself in studies and activities and struggle to immerse myself in the key relationships of my life.

The issue of diligence will take a different shape for each of us. But the subtle call of our culture to laziness invites us to death. Biblical diligence guides us to life.

Chapter Eighteen

Life Sucks

Pessimism Clashes with Optimism

Two shoe salesmen went to a remote area in Africa to scout out new market possibilities. After several weeks, the home office received word from each man. The first sent a brief note: "No one here wears shoes. No market exists. We'll need to look elsewhere." The other reported, "Send a shipload of shoes as quickly as possible. No one here wears shoes—yet."

We find optimists and pessimists all over the world. Some people see the glass as half full while others see it as half empty. Winston Churchill once observed, "An optimist sees an opportunity in every calamity; a pessimist sees a calamity in every opportunity." Negative thinking, however, increases in our culture as people grow disillusioned, cynical, and skeptical. Most of us in one way or another express some negativity. An optimist in one area of life—perhaps our capacity to earn money—may be a pessimist in another area—perhaps our effectiveness as a parent.

We may embrace pessimism due to a variety of reasons: race or gender discrimination, education level, socioeconomic status, workplace politics, or even our personality. Many of us consequently lose confidence in our personal futures.

CULTURE'S VALUE

What It Is

In 1911, Ambrose Bierce, a journalist and short story writer, humorously defined pessimism as, "a philosophy forced upon the convictions of the observer by the disheartening prevalence of the optimist with his scarecrow hope and his unsightly smile." Bierce obviously didn't appreciate the "unsightly smile." Pessimism transcends philosophy and has become a method to avoid dashed hopes. Shoot low or shoot at nothing and you'll be safer. Pessimism has, as a result, become integral to our mainstream culture. The optimist sees it as resignation and defeat, but the pessimist sees it as realism and common sense.

It's for Real

The futility of life for some leads to pessimism, but for others, life simply lacks hope. Prisons, slums, and oppressed people groups therefore provide prolific breeding grounds for hopelessness. Dorothy, an Australian aborigine, has been the target of racial slurs and taunts all her life, mostly from non-aboriginal people. But even family members chided her for being so daring and outrageous as to plan a big trip to the

USA in 2002. Her pessimistic peers wanted to stomp on her big dreams and high hopes.

We also see pessimism among the wealthy. King Solomon of ancient Israel declared, "Everything is futile and vain" (see Eccl. 1:2 NASB). Many of today's most successful individuals have battled despondency. Kurt Cobain, the late lead singer of the rock band Nirvana, shocked the world when he committed suicide in 1994. Celebrity suicides seem all too common.

Pessimism has become common even in the church. We frequently hear phrases such as, "We can't do that," or "It's no use." We doubt that God will resolve our problems, that people will change, or that we can grow. We are full of pessimism about the church's effectiveness, leadership, and future.

In a similar manner, pessimism dogs our marriages. Many couples have no confidence that their brittle relationships will last or that they can clear the rocky terrain that has become their home. They don't expect improvement, and they see mutual love and care as unrealistic.

Pessimism and despair, hopelessness and futility impact people without regard for race, wealth, or gender. Yet paradoxically, we often embrace pessimism because of its payoffs.

The Payoffs

As one cynic has observed, "It's better to be a delighted pessimist than a disappointed optimist." Pessimism offers *safe haven*. It lacks adventure but also reduces risk. We don't have to deal with as much pain of failure if we attempt little and expect less. One influential Christian statesman claims to have a pessimistic view of people so he can be joyfully surprised when folk rise above his low expectations.

Christopher Robin's friends in the Hundred Acre Wood highlight the benefits. Winnie the Pooh, Tigger, and Piglet are excitable, hopeful, and optimistic. But they get into trouble and confusion with their simple minds. Those who really think, know better. Like Eeyore the donkey. Everything for him is glum and gray. But since he always expects the worst, *he experiences few disappointments in life.* Of course, his whole life is a disappointment. But at least his pessimism produces stability.

The Costs

Helen Keller, struck deaf and blind when only nineteen months old, possessed a sharp mind trapped inside a broken body. With the help of a close friend and teacher, Anne Sullivan, she learned to communicate. Helen once said, "No pessimist ever discovered the secrets of the stars, or sailed to an uncharted land, or opened a new heaven to the human spirit." When we subdue hope, *we limit our willingness to risk*, which ultimately diminishes our destiny. Henry Ford put it another way: "If you think you can do a thing or you think you can't do a thing, you're right."

But pessimism also *affects us internally.* Pessimists tend to criticize everything and everyone around them. Fear dominates their lives. Short-sighted, they to some degree embrace the famous dictum, "Eat, drink, and be merry, for tomorrow we die." Psychologists use a variety of words to describe the negative thinker: rigid, one-sided, close-minded, and narrow.

Pessimism, as safe as it feels, *denies possibilities*. It closes doors and overlooks options. It lacks creativity and rejects pioneering. It fails to dream, ultimately sucking the hope and life out of others. The phrase, "life sucks," which expresses the pessimist fairly well, ironically becomes, "we suck out life." Life becomes paralyzed.

GOD'S VALUE

What It Is

Six centuries before Jesus, God gave a vision to the prophet Ezekiel. Ezekiel saw a valley of dry bones that represented the nation of Israel in exile. The people were saying, "Our bones are dried up and our hope has perished. We are completely cut off" (Ezek. 37:11 NASB). Pessimism dries our bones, drains us of life, and flourishes in the absence of hope. We feel cut off.

Godly hope stands in stark contrast to pessimism. This hope is neither wishful thinking nor fanciful imagination; it is a confidence and certainty in the goodness of God, the potential of his people, and the security of our future. It ought to pervade the life of the believer.

It's for Real

Hope permeates the Bible. We have a "God of hope" (Rom. 15:13). We were formerly "without hope and without God in the world" (Eph. 2:12) but have now been "born again to a living hope" (1 Peter 1:3). We, therefore, "rejoice in hope" (Rom. 5:2) because this "hope does not disappoint" (Rom. 5:5). We hold fast to "the hope of the gospel" (Col. 1:23) and wear "as a helmet, the hope of salvation" (1 Thess. 5:8). The psalmist said, "How blessed is he ... whose hope is in the LORD" (Ps. 146:5).

Two glimmering facets of Godly hope stand out. First, we have *hope for eternity.* The apostle Paul talked about "the hope of eternal life" (Titus 1:2). Whatever happens now, whether for good or ill, the future looks far better because God himself holds the future. Nothing in this life can separate us from the love of God that we receive through Christ Jesus (see Rom. 8:39). We can look forward with confidence to the future. Alexander Pope put it this way:

> Hope springs eternal in the human breast;
> Man never is, but always to be blest:
> The soul, uneasy and confin'd from home,
> Rests and expatiates in a life to come.

Second, we have *hope in the present.* "If God is for us, who can be against us?" (Rom. 8:31). If nothing can take away our hope for eternity, then we have the greatest security for the present. The writer to the Hebrews eloquently makes this point when he writes, "Faith is being sure of what we hope for ..." (11:1). He then gives example after example of men and women who had this hope in God and endured. Hope dramatically shaped their lives. They had direction, purpose, and conviction. God offers the same hope to us.

The Payoffs

Rather than "sucking," this biblical hope produces *inner peace and strength.* Todd Beamer boarded United Flight 93, which crashed in a Pennsylvania field on September 11, 2002. Lisa Jefferson, a supervisor with GTE Airfone Customer Care Center, spoke with Todd just before he and other passengers attacked the hijackers and prevented the plane from crashing into a building filled with people.

She recalled him saying, "We're going to do something.... I don't think we're going to get out of this thing. I'm going to have to go out on faith."

Her response? "If I hadn't known it was a real hijacking, I'd have thought it was a crank call, because Todd was so rational and methodical about what he was doing."

How could Todd face death with such a calm? Hope in Christ produces courage and resilience. It equips us with boldness and strength when we face temptations to cave in. It produces an unconquerable inner peace and strength.

The Costs

When we approach life with such a biblical mindset, we *shine in the darkness*. People who prefer the darkness of pessimism rarely enjoy the light of hope. They prefer to drag others down rather than to rise up from their gloom. Pessimism and hope are two incompatible approaches to life. They clash with each other.

Hope costs because it requires *risk taking*. Rick believed God wanted him to start a church in Southern California. He arrived there in 1979 with a wife and daughter, a U-Haul, no home or place to begin services, and no money. Only by maxing out his credit cards could he get started. Quite a risk. One that many of us wouldn't dare attempt. He took the risk during his first Sunday worship service to express the dream God had given him: to build a church of 20,000 members that would start a daughter church each year.

Since then, Saddleback Valley Community Church has started thirty daughter churches. Rick Warren took huge risks because he had confidence that God had called him and would be faithful to follow through on his part.

When we genuinely believe that God keeps his promises, we'll take a risk talking about him because we believe transformation can happen. When we believe that not even God can reach a person—"It can't be done"—we won't risk that person's refusal to accept Christ. When we believe God, though, our confidence and certainty push us forward until we succeed.

LIVING IT OUT

What does having this hope mean for our lives? It means that we don't give up on our marriages when tough times come. If we have real confidence in the power of God, then we cling tightly to a deep hope for reconciliation, restoration, transformation, and glory. We ought not consider this a mandate to remain in an abusive or dangerous relationship, but most of us don't find ourselves in abusive relationships. We're simply bored or frustrated with our spouse. We simply need a fresh perspective by ditching pessimism and embracing biblical hope.

Hope also means that we expect the best from people. We will often get it. When I (David) first came to teach in the

United States, a colleague kindly warned me about the weaknesses and foibles of other faculty members. If I had listened to the gossip, I would have approached everyone with cynicism and suspicion. I chose instead to believe the best about people and delightedly found that many of the reported flaws were gross exaggerations. These colleagues were wonderful people with enormous potential.

Many years ago, a wise old pastor made this statement: "You cannot minister to those of whom you are critical." Expect the best from people. See their strengths and potential, not their flaws and failures. When you expect the best, you will often receive what you've hoped for. The ministry opportunities that emerge will amaze us.

Finally, hope means that we don't approach our future with fear or insecurity because we know that God holds us in his hands. Hope takes away the sting of death. The apostle Paul wrote, "O death, where is your victory? O death, where is your sting?" (1 Cor. 15:55 NASB). Our hope in the work of Christ enables us to see death for what it is: not the end, but a transition; not the final experience, but the gateway to eternity. We can face it—despite the grief and pain of separation—not with fear, but with courage.

A God-centered hope firms our faith and allows us to love God, ourselves, and others. Paul said, "And now these three remain: faith, hope and love. But the greatest of these is love" (1 Cor. 13:13). Yes, love is the greatest, but we find hope in the middle of everything.

Chapter Nineteen

What Will Be Will Be

Determinism Clashes with Our Choice

I (Tim) grew up with the beaches of Southern California, but the mountains lived in my heart. When I led a month-long mission project to the small New Mexico mountain village of Penasco, I felt like I'd come home. A year later, back in California, I decided to settle down somewhere in the mountains. I committed to spend only three days looking for a job in Taos, not far from Penasco, before heading to a possibility in Colorado. Not many jobs were available in Taos.

I stopped along the way to enjoy a fine Saturday dinner in Albuquerque, then drove two more hours to Taos to go dancing. I passed a nice little adobe church in town and decided to worship there the next morning, where I met the pastor, Phil McClendon. We hit it off well enough for him to ask me if a part-time ministry job would interest me. It did, but I mentioned to him my three-day timetable. The pastor said, "I'll see what I can do."

I visited friends in Penasco on Monday and called Phil Tuesday morning. Phil's wife, Jackie, said he'd found a job opening. Someone needed a caretaker for an unused guest ranch, and Phil was "downtown somewhere." I drove downtown, parked, looked up, and Phil stood ten feet away. That never happened again! Phil explained how a couple in the church had just sold the ranch and the new east coast owner wanted them to hire someone to live there.

The former owners, however, had gone to the airport. So Phil took me to meet an Indian artist at his "office," a local bar. To their great surprise, they found the former owners eating lunch there. They'd returned early from the airport.

They described the job and set an appointment for 4 PM I, being a little anxious, arrived early, got the royal tour, they offered the job and I accepted it. Within a minute, the phone rang. The owner had previously offered the job to someone else, but he hadn't been ready to accept it. Now, at 3:55 PM, he was. Just a little too late.

That job changed the course of my life. I got involved with the church, where the pastor repeatedly challenged me to consider a return to vocational ministry, which I eventually did. I later counted in this complex of events at least nine "coincidences." If even one had gone another way, the end result would have been much different, and my life-changing sojourn in Taos would never have happened.

I thought I freely made each choice. I realize in retrospect, however, that God orchestrated all of those events to reach his goal for my life. Both realities seemed true. But how could that be?

CULTURE'S VALUE

What It Is

The *Cambridge International Dictionary* defines determinism as, "the theory which states that everything that happens must happen the way it does and could not have happened any other way." Some call that fatalism, which *Webster's Revised Unabridged Dictionary* defines as, "the doctrine that all things are subject to fate, or that they take place by inevitable necessity."

Que sera, sera. Whatever will be, will be. The "fates" have determined it. When God punches your ticket, you're out of here.

It's for Real

Determinism permeates our society in at least three different ways. Advocates of the first version believe that *cosmic forces determine our destiny*, and we have little say at all in it. We see evidence of this in the widespread interest in horoscopes, palm readings, crystals, tarot cards, and clairvoyance. Such people would say, "What do you expect? I'm a Pisces." Or, "The devil made me do it!"

Devotees of the second viewpoint to our genes as the basis of determinism. The message is that *our genetic makeup rules our lives*. Thus, I'm alcoholic or gay because my genes predetermined my course of action, not because I choose it.

The third view of determinism appeals to *nurture* as the basis of our behavior. It is *our upbringing that controls us.* I beat my wife because I saw it in my family of origin. I'm not to blame. I get angry because my parents failed me. I'm not responsible. If I sexually abuse someone, it's because uncle Harry abused *me* as a child. What else would you expect?

Even in the church, we find extreme forms of determinism that state that God chooses who comes to Christ, that all things happen according to his will. No one can stand against what God wants to accomplish. And we can cite biblical passages that support our position. Do we control the length of our lives? Job 14:5 proves our point: "Man's days are determined; you [O God] have decreed the number of his months and have set limits he cannot exceed."

In a culture that appeals to "diminished responsibility," determinism is attractive. We do what we do because of others, or God, or fate. We're not responsible. We can blame others for what we do.

The Payoffs

The first benefit of determinism is that it *decreases personal responsibility.* Since other forces cause our actions, they are to blame. We're free of guilt. Many embrace determinism for this reason. It gives us a loophole, an out. If it's not my fault, then you may neither punish me nor think less of me. When a relationship fails, we can shrug and say, "It wasn't meant to be," and we absolve ourselves from contributing to the failure.

A second benefit of determinism is that it *encourages risk-taking*. Since our fate has been set, we can take dangerous risks. We can't lose, unless it was "meant to be." If we try and fail, it was in the cards anyway. And if the risk brings a good result, that outcome reinforces our belief in determinism. I might wager my house at the casino because if "Lady Luck" smiles on me, I'll win. If she doesn't, I'm likely to lose the house anyway. Crazy thinking, but it happens.

The Costs

Let's flip each of those advantages to reveal the disadvantages. The failure to take personal responsibility is actually a *failure to mature*. When we blame rogue forces for our actions, we experience a profound breakdown in relationships and community. When Adam blamed Eve for giving him the forbidden fruit and Eve blamed the serpent— "It wasn't my fault; they made me do it"—they became alienated from God and from each other. A high cost.

We find heightened hopelessness on the flip side of increased risk-taking. The pessimism of our previous chapter is linked to determinism. "Nothing I do will make a difference" implies determinism and hopelessness. While some people become reckless and dangerous, other people despair.

GOD'S VALUE

What It Is

In contrast to living like puppets dangling on the strings of fate, God offers the freedom to make moral choices. While recognizing that outside forces can *influence* us, we also realize they do not arbitrarily *control* us. We retain the ability to make decisions. We set the course of our lives. That means we must take personal responsibility for our choices, regardless of the degree to which others influence us. We're accountable for the ways we respond and for the decisions we make.

It's for Real

The Bible states that God created us with the marvelous gift of choice. Adam and Eve chose names for the animals. They were also free to choose their destiny by either obeying or disobeying God. God influenced and Satan tempted, but *they* chose.

A classic passage in the Bible later describes how the Jewish leader Joshua challenged God's people to be clear in their commitment to the Lord:

> Now fear the LORD and serve him with all
> faithfulness. Throw away the gods your
> forefathers worshiped beyond the River and in
> Egypt, and serve the LORD. But if serving the
> LORD seems undesirable to you, *then choose for*
> *yourselves* this day whom you will serve, whether
> the gods your forefathers served beyond the River,
> or the gods of the Amorites, in whose land you are
> living. But as for me and my household, we will
> serve the LORD (Josh. 24:14–15, emphasis added).

Joshua chose to serve God and encouraged the people to make the same choice. Other elements of choice flow throughout the Bible. Romans 10:9–10 sets forth our freedom to confess and believe: "If you confess with your mouth, 'Jesus is Lord,' and believe in your heart that God raised him from the dead, you will be saved. For it is with your heart that you believe and are justified, and it is with your mouth that you confess and are saved."

We choose to make a verbal confession. We choose to believe. Now, please think carefully about the implications. If we choose, then we bear responsibility for those choices. If we choose wrongly, we (and others) suffer. If we choose correctly, we (and others) benefit.

Take this a step further, a step that will strike a balance between absolute determinism and absolute free choice. Our decisions influence and are influenced by others. Although we can make free moral decisions, we're not completely independent. We live in an interconnected world.

First, the decisions of others influence us. Jesus said, "But if anyone causes one of these little ones who believe in me to sin, it would be better for him to have a large millstone hung around his neck and to be drowned in the depths of the sea" (Matt. 18:6).

Similarly, we affect others. If Harold decides to leave his wife for another woman, he limits her ability to choose marriage with him. She chooses how to respond to his choice, but his choice limits her future choices. Their lives are interconnected.

Second, God plays a major role in our lives, while allowing us great choice. For example, God "wants all men to be saved and to come to a knowledge of the truth" (1 Tim. 2:4).

Has God determined that all will follow his will? Many verses in the Bible indicate that not all people will be saved, but not because God doesn't want them to be saved. They, themselves, choose to reject God.

Some people go to hell, in violation of God's will. God doesn't compel us to do what he would like us to do. Neither does he ignore us. He cajoles us, calls us, and convicts us. He even chooses us, the Bible says. But we must also choose him.

God does not hold us on a string. He does, however, participate in our lives. Rather than determining our choices, he works alongside us to influence and empower our choices. 1 Corinthians 10:13, for example, tells us, "No temptation has seized you except what is common to man. And God is faithful; he will not let you be tempted beyond what you can bear. But when you are tempted, he will also provide a way out so that you can stand up under it." God empowers and enables our decisions, but he does not make our choices for us.

Romans 8:28 tells us he also maximizes positive outcomes: "And we know that in all things God works for the good of those who love him, who have been called according to his purpose." God promises, even when evil comes our way, to work for good in it. He influences the impact that evil has on us.

We make real choices. We have the responsibility to make moral decisions. God involves himself in our lives but doesn't override what we decide.

The Payoffs

When we understand that we can make moral choices, we realize *our lives have significance*. We make real choices. We can have a positive impact on others, our culture, and the kingdom of God. We can make a difference by what we choose to do. That opens up a wide variety of avenues for our lives to become meaningful change agents. What a wonderful realization. The gift of choice lends new potential and significance to every life.

The gift of choice also allows us *truly to love*. A mechanistic, deterministic universe renders love an illusion. If we *have to* love someone, we are little more than programmed robots. The kingdom of God doesn't utilize programmed robots but empowered people. We can rise above the values of the world to love each other deeply in community.

The Costs

The ability to choose, however, *forces us to choose*. We can't avoid making moral decisions by assuming that what we choose makes no difference. Just as determinism eliminates or decreases moral choices, free will requires them.

Choice means we become *responsible for consequences*. We can't slide through life, refusing to take responsibility for our actions. We cannot constantly blame others for our circumstances. We have to accept our bad decisions.

LIVING IT OUT

The personal story that opened this chapter illustrates that God clearly has a general will for each Christian—that we accept salvation and grow in maturity. He also has specific desires, like establishing me (Tim) at the ranch in Taos. Others make choices that shape, enhance, and affect our lives. Many choices beyond our own influence our lives. We can find a wonder and a mystery in all of that: The interaction of so many wills—God's, ours, and others'—works together to create the tapestry we call life.

But we do make real decisions, and we choose how we respond to the situations we face. We shape our lives by our choices. Our choices possess real power.

Second, if God has given us the gift of choice and free will, should we not also extend that to each other? This has an impact on marriage—respecting each other's choices; parenting—allowing children increasingly to exercise freedom of choice; the workplace—freeing people to make decisions without constantly overriding them.

Even when striving to do our best as imperfect free moral agents, we'll inevitably make bad decisions. We won't always act ethically. We'll cause pain for others. How should we respond? We must own up to it, acknowledging that we did wrong—both to God and to people. We then strive to avoid that mistake in the future. We will make restitution, fixing the wrong we did.

Finally, we *leave room for God.* God loves and knows us best. We make choices, tentatively at times. We say, "God, from praying, studying, and getting advice, I think this looks like the best course to take. If so, please let it happen. If not, please shut it down."

We and God operate as a partnership in our spiritual agenda. We take action; God brings results. "I planted the seed, Apollos watered it, but God made it grow. So neither he who plants nor he who waters is anything, but only God, who makes things grow" (1 Cor. 3:6–7).

We choose to live by kingdom values, then we leave room for God to do as he desires.

We must, in conclusion, understand the importance of free choice. We make choices between the values of the world and the values of the kingdom of God. We choose how we will live. We choose how to respond to the people in our lives.

God has determined the ideal boundaries that enable us to live our lives to the full, but he does not force us to remain within those boundaries. The culture of our day has sadly chosen to ignore God's boundaries and has developed, to its harm, its own boundaries. The kingdom of God, in every sense of the word, must be countercultural. What does that require of us?

NexStep

Just Leave God Out of It

*A study guide for personal reflection
or group discussion*

Chapter 1

1. Identify evidence of secularism in your own school, workplace, or community.

2. Analyze a 30-minute sitcom on television and write down the values you see expressed (for example, honesty, purity, selflessness, cooperation, and so forth, or their opposites). Sitcoms tend to be exaggerated but not offensive snapshots of our culture. What does the show teach you about our culture? How was God portrayed, if at all?

3. From your experience, make a list of the damage that secularism is causing.

4. What might be some of the personal costs for you in rejecting secularism and embracing the reality of God?

5. What are three ways in which you could live more aware of God and his kingdom this week?

Chapter 2

1. Identify some examples from your own life this week when you have been tempted to do something by the phrases "everyone is doing it" or "I just want to do it" or "who will know" or "it won't hurt anyone". These are probably examples of relativism.

2. How have you been affected by people who do what is "right in their own eyes" and let go of a common set of standards?

3. Study Genesis 1–3 and make a list of the principles that emerge from those first stories of the Bible. If we were back in Eden today, how would we live and what would God sanction as good and right?

4. Read Jesus' Sermon on the Mount in Matthew 5–7. What moral principles stand out for you from that remarkable passage?

5. How will you identify the difference between moral absolutes and personal preferences?

Chapter 3

1. How do you feel about "other religions"?

2. When have you faced the pressure to accept pluralism?

3. What examples of pluralism have you seen in your school, workplace, or neighborhood?

4. How can Christians be exclusivist about Christ without being antagonistic? Is it possible?

5. Read a religion article from a secular newspaper or popular magazine and look for underlying core values. Is pluralism dominant? Is it presumed?

Chapter 4

1. What damage has self-centeredness done to your life?

2. What most impresses you about how Jesus used his life to serve others?

3. How have you served someone in this past week or two?

4. How has it benefited your life? Describe what happened.

5. What two practical steps can you take this week to increase your service to others?

Chapter 5

1. Do you agree that independence is a deeply ingrained part of our culture?

2. How has it personally affected you?

3. When, where, and how do you rely on other people and, conversely, give support to other people? If you don't depend on others, what are your reasons?

4. How can you enhance the "community," which is your local church?

5. What will you do differently this week to foster interdependence in your marriage, family, small group, or workplace?

6. Read Acts 2:42. What four practices were a part of the church's daily life? How did those practices build interdependence?

Chapter 6

1. Read Philippians 2:1–4. What are the key phrases and how do they relate to this topic?

2. In what areas of your life are you the most competitive? Sports, work, grades, reputation, relationships, etc?

3. How do you feel about winning and losing?

4. What are some ways that a competitive spirit has affected your life?

5. How can *you* turn your competitive feelings into a cooperative mindset?

6. What are some specific actions you might take this week to help *others* (in your family or school or workplace) become less competitive?

Chapter 7

1. A *U.S. News & World Report* article in May 2002 asked the question, "What is sex?" It noted that "kids don't seem to view many sexual behaviors as *real* sex." For example, 50 percent of all teens don't consider oral sex, *sex*. What constitutes sexual behavior and where should the lines be drawn in the pursuit of purity?

2. Why did you answer the previous question as you did?

3. Over 50 percent of teens say that their parents "rarely" or "never" speak to them about sex. How can Christian parents more openly discuss sex and promote purity? If you have an open and frank relationship with your kids, how did you achieve it and how do you sustain it?

4. What are some other practical ways to pursue and preserve purity in this sex-saturated society?

Chapter 8

1. Read 1 Corinthians 5:1–13. What principles of tough love can you identify?

2. What principles from the aforementioned passage do you struggle to apply?

3. Think of a time when another person lovingly confronted you. Judgmentally confronted you. How did you feel during and after the encounter(s)?

4. When have you confronted another Christian? Describe what happened and what you would do differently.

5. Name some relationships in which you need to apply this chapter. How do you plan to do that?

Chapter 9

1. Make a list of various slogans in the media and on the street. Categorize them according to "instant satisfaction" or "delayed gratification." What can you learn from this?

2. How do you feel when you have to wait for something that you want, especially when other people may already have it or are experiencing it?

3. What benefits have you experienced from delayed gratification?

4. What challenges are you facing today in this area? Think of home improvements, clothes, food, entertainment, career, money, sex, and other things.

5. What do you believe are wise decisions to make, in light of this chapter? Why?

Chapter 10

1. Think of a time when you sacrificed your own plans or desires but found joy in serving someone else. Describe it.

2. How were you able to see God's hand in that experience?

3. Identify some of the pleasures that have had a negative impact in your life. What sacrifices will be necessary to produce lasting, positive results?

4. What are the connections between hedonism and self-centeredness (chapter 4), sexual freedom (chapter 7), tolerance (chapter 8), and instant satisfaction (chapter 9)?

5. How can we swim against the tide when our culture is so devoted to the pursuit of pleasure? What are some practical steps?

Chapter 11

1. Read the entire passage of Ephesians 5:21–6:9. With which relationships do you most struggle in the practice of submission? Why?

2. What types of power do you typically use to get your way?—intellectual, physical, emotional, or financial?

3. When have others told you that you are manipulative? Were they right? Describe the situation and what you learned from it.

4. What specific steps can you take this week to develop a more submissive mindset and actions? Why is the cultivation of a submissive heart a desirable discipline?

Chapter 12

1. Read 2 Corinthians 10:5. What does this tell you about how our thought life impacts obedience and pragmatism?

2. Describe a time when you achieved a good outcome by questionable means.

3. How does pragmatism hurt your walk with God?

4. Why is obedience such a tough task for believers today?

5. What can you do this week to become more obedient?

Chapter 13

1. What do you dream of "achieving" with your life?

2. How has ambition affected your family, past and present?

3. What are some symptoms of ambition?

4. What are some ways to counteract ambition in your life?

5. What two steps can you take this week to help make your highest goal to honor God? What will it cost you? What do you expect the outcome to be?

Chapter 14

1. Read 1 Samuel 15:1–23. What, in your own words, is God's standard of success? How does this affect your life?

2. To which cultural standards of success are you most vulnerable? Why? Provide an example.

3. Has the happiness of our society increased as we've experienced so much material and technological success? Why?

4. In what ways are you most tempted to keep score?

5. What keeps you from being faithful to God? Why?

6. What specific steps can you take this week to be more faithful to God?

Chapter 15

1. Read Psalm 24:1–2. What does this tell you about accumulating earthly goods?

2. Read 2 Corinthians 8 and 9. What principles about giving strike you as important for your life?

3. What aspects of your life may indicate that you have adopted the culture's value of accumulating wealth?

4. Describe an experience of giving "what you can't afford to give." How did it work out? How has it changed your values?

5. What specific steps can you take this week to incorporate more sacrificial giving into your life?

6. As we consider lifestyles of nonaccumulation, what role does sharing play? How might sharing resources (with family, friends, and neighbors) help address the drive to accumulate, and what are some of the things you can share with others?

Chapter 16

1. Read 1 Timothy 6:6–11. What impresses you the most in this passage?

2. What are some examples of consumerism in your life or community?

3. How do you emotionally respond to the kingdom value of simple living?

4. What are some ways in which you might simplify your own lifestyle and consume less?

5. How will you distribute the resources you gather through simpler living?

6. How can we be sure that simplicity springs out of contentment and not guilt? And what difference does that make?

Chapter 17

1. In what areas do you find it most difficult to be diligent?

2. Do you work hard but struggle to complete tasks? Why do you think that is?

3. Describe your attitude toward work. Is it a curse, a blessing, or something in between? Give an example and discuss this.

4. Name three primary goals you have for your life. How can you relate God's value of diligence to them?

5. What steps can you take this week to become more diligent?

Chapter 18

1. How would you describe yourself—as a pessimist or an optimist? Rate yourself on a scale of 1–10, with 1 being utterly defeated and 10 being utterly irrepressible.

2. How would you have rated ten years ago? What does this say to you?

3. Has your disposition been a conscious choice or the product of experiences, personality, and the influence of people around you?

4. In what one area of your life would hope make an immediate difference?

5. How might you move up one notch on the hope scale this week?

Chapter 19

1. What most perplexes you about the clash between determinism and free will?

2. Before reading this chapter, toward which of the two did you mostly lean? Have you changed your view? If so, in what way?

3. Describe an experience you may have had that was similar to the one Tim shared in the introduction to this chapter, where God has seemed to guide your choices. Describe the situation and its results, and how you felt during and after it.

4. Describe a time in which you have fatalistically taken unwise risks. Are you as apt to do so now? Why?

5. How will this chapter affect your life this week?

6. How have the principles of this book changed the way you look at our culture?

7. What can you do to be a countercultural change agent?

1. *U.S. News & World Report*, May 6, 2002, 42.

2. www.pluralism.org

3. *Washington Post*, Sunday, Feb 22, 1998, A1

4. *Los Angeles Times*, Orange County Edition, Sunday, Dec 22, 2002, B17

5. Osterbrock, Donald, *Yerkes Observatory, 1892–1950: The Birth, Near Death, and Resurrection of a Scientific Research Institution*, Chicago University Press, 1997.

6. *Daily Telegraph*, London, Tuesday, July 9, 2002.

7. CBSNEWS.com, Washington, Sept 26, 2002.

8. *U.S. News & World Report*, May 27, 2002, 44

The Word at Work . . .

*W*hat would you do if you wanted to share God's love with children on the streets of your city? That's the dilemma David C. Cook faced in 1870s Chicago. His answer was to create literature that would capture children's hearts.

Out of those humble beginnings grew a worldwide ministry that has used literature to proclaim God's love and disciple generation after generation. Cook Communications Ministries is committed to personal discipleship—to helping people of all ages learn God's Word, embrace his salvation, walk in his ways, and minister in his name.

Opportunities—and Crisis

We live in a land of plenty—including plenty of Christian literature! But what about the rest of the world? Jesus commanded, "Go and make disciples of all nations" (Matt. 28:19) and we want to obey this commandment. But how does a publishing organization "go" into all the world?

There are five times as many Christians around the world as there are in North America. Christian workers in many of these countries have no more than a New Testament, or perhaps a single shared copy of the Bible, from which to learn and teach.

We are committed to sharing what God has given us with such Christians.

A vital part of Cook Communications Ministries is our international outreach, Cook Communications Ministries International (CCMI). Your purchase of this book, and of other books and Christian-growth products from Cook, enables CCMI to provide Bibles and Christian literature to people in more than 150 languages in 65 countries.

Cook Communications Ministries is a not-for-profit, self-supporting organization. Revenues from sales of our books, Bible curriculum, and other church and home products not only fund our U.S. ministry, but also fund our CCMI ministry around the world. One hundred percent of donations to CCMI go to our international literature programs.

...Around the World

CCMI reaches out internationally in three ways:

· Our premier International Christian Publishing Institute (ICPI) trains leaders from nationally led publishing houses around the world to develop evangelism and discipleship materials to transform lives in their countries.

· We provide literature for pastors, evangelists, and Christian workers in their national language. We provide study helps for pastors and lay leaders in many parts of the world, such as China, India, Cuba, Iran, and Vietnam.

· We reach people at risk—refugees, AIDS victims, street children, and famine victims—with God's Word. CCMI puts literature that shares the Good News into the hands of people at spiritual risk—people who might die before they hear the name of Jesus and are transformed by his love.

Word Power—God's Power

Faith Kidz, RiverOak, Honor, Life Journey, Victor, NexGen — every time you purchase a book produced by Cook Communications Ministries, you not only meet a vital personal need in your life or in the life of someone you love, but you're also a part of ministering to José in Colombia, Humberto in Chile, Gousa in India, or Lidiane in Brazil. You help make it possible for a pastor in China, a child in Peru, or a mother in West Africa to enjoy a life-changing book. And because you helped, children and adults around the world are learning God's Word and walking in his ways.

Thank you for your partnership in helping to disciple the world. May God bless you with the power of his Word in your life.

For more information about our international ministries, visit www.ccmi.org.